Capture the Moment

Building Faith Traditions for Families

Rick & Sue Isbell

DISCIPLESHIP RESOURCES

P.O. BOX 840 • NASHVILLE, TENNESSEE 37202-0840

www.discipleshipresources.org

Library of Congress Card Catalog No. 97-066576

ISBN 0-88177-225-9

DR225

Table of Contents

1999

123927

Introduction

Writing *Capture the Moment* has been a time of great reflection, catharsis, and adventure. As we considered the spectrum of events to be covered in these pages, we realized how very typical we are. We were somewhat amazed to discover that all of the life events in this book are familiar, either in our own family experiences or in those of our friends. In either instance, we have found three things to be true: God is present in every aspect of our lives—good, bad, and in between; our family has been strengthened by facing both the happy times and the discouraging times together; and we are not the first, nor will we be the last, family unit to live through many of the celebrations and struggles life has to offer.

Life is full of obvious times for celebration. Each May, we celebrate the anniversary of our marriage. With great joy and thankfulness, we recall when our daughters were born. Birthdays, graduations, baptisms, and confirmations have also been occasions for family rejoicing throughout the years.

Mixed with the great joys of life have come times of discouragement and sorrow. Coping with the deaths of our parents, living through traumatic job loss and the resultant relocation of our family, struggling with colleagues as they went through divorces—all of these experiences have significantly affected us as individuals and as a family unit. Sandwiched somewhere in between the highs and the lows are events that we wish we had enjoyed a little longer or celebrated a little more: family vacations, giving and receiving a first allowance, living with our first cat and dog, the loss of a child's first tooth. These are times that seemed so ordinary when they occurred. It took years of reflection for us to realize how special they truly were.

Capture the Moment is designed to help families celebrate the good times, find strength in the discouraging times, and preserve the memories of the times in between. All of life is a gift from God.

The chapters of this book focus on milestones an average family may experience throughout its life journey. Each chapter links "real world" life significance with biblical background to give readers both practical and spiritual guidance as they bring their families together for celebration or reflection. Ideas for celebration and for discussion starters have been included to serve as a springboard for individualizing each topic.

Capture the Moment could not have been written without our recollections of experiences. Many of these are shared in the devotions at the end of each chapter. Our children, our parents, our extended family, our friends, and our congregation have been significant in our faith journeys, and they are reflected in the stories. As we included them in the writing of this book, we realized that we are no different from anyone who reads this book: We are ordinary people who want to capture, cherish, and remember the extraordinary times in our lives.

Capture the Moment is written primarily for use by families in the home. Ideas for use in small group settings and in other church settings can be found in the back of the book.

A particular word of thanks needs to go to a group of people who came together early in the planning of *Capture the Moment*. They helped us identify the moments we would write about and offered advice and suggestions from their unique perspectives. This group also reviewed the completed manuscript, providing valuable comments that improved the finished product.

Members of this group are:
- Geumhee Cho from Nashville, Tennessee
- Myrtle Felkner from Centerville, Iowa
- Lia Icaza-Willetts from Nashville, Tennessee
- Nelida Morales from Miami, Florida
- Diane Olson from Chicago, Illinois
- MaryJane Pierce Norton from Nashville, Tennessee
- Jacqueline Rose-Tucker from Atlanta, Georgia

Capture the Moment

1 ▪ Becoming a Parent

Being a parent for the first time is a life-changing experience. No matter if you have waited nine months or ten years for the birth or the adoption, you never forget the day you welcome your first child into your life. It is a joyous, anxious, and humbling event that forever changes you. Being responsible for and influencing the physical, emotional, and social well-being of an individual for the next eighteen to twenty years cannot be taken lightly. However, sharing in the life experiences of a child is a joy without comparison.

The first child brings unique experiences because parents are learning how to be parents. Even if countless books are read and courses are taken, being a first-time parent involves on-the-job learning.

Welcoming the first child into the family can mean different things to different people: It can mean the fulfillment of years of trying and waiting; it can mean rearranging a previously imagined life plan; it can be the end of a long and difficult pregnancy or it can be the day that the adoption paperwork ends, and the child comes home; it can bring joy as dreams are realized. The individual meanings may differ, but the common truth is that having a child changes the home dynamics—from one with primarily adult relationships and schedules to one made up of a child and adults relating and living together.

▪ From Our Faith Roots

In the Bible we find stories of first-time parents, both birth parents and adoptive parents. In Exodus 2:1-10 we read about the birth of Moses. After his birth, his biological mother gave him up to save his life. Even though his birth mother loved Moses, she knew it was better that he not remain with her. Moses was found and adopted by the daughter of the Egyptian pharaoh.

In Luke 1:5-80 we find the story of the birth of John the Baptist. Elizabeth and Zechariah were good people and had lived righteous lives. They had done everything that was expected of them by the commandments. Yet they were disappointed that they had been unable to conceive a child. (The Hebrew culture considered not being able to have children as a sign of God's displeasure.) Convinced that they were past the age of childbearing, Zechariah and Elizabeth were ecstatic and yet unbelieving when they discovered that they were to become parents. When their son John was born, everyone, including the neighbors and relatives, rejoiced.

These two stories convey some of the situations and feelings that parents experience today. Adoptive parents may or may not know the biological parents of their child. Sometimes biological parents must give up their child because of situations beyond their control. We can understand the feelings that both Moses' birth mother and adoptive mother must have experienced.

Elizabeth and Zechariah demonstrate the many feelings and emotions of first-time parents. We recognize the feelings of frustration and anxiety as the couple longed for a child of their own. We can even identify with Zechariah when he questions God about Elizabeth having a son. But the overriding emotions shared in this story are joy and happiness—not only by the parents but also by the neighbors and relatives. Isn't this the way it is today?

The common denominator in both of these biblical stories is that God is active and present. Whatever adversities or situations the parents face or the feelings they have, God is in control and only wants the best for both parent and child. Even when the situation fails to turn out the way it was planned or even when we question God about being parents, it is comforting to know that God is with us. God knows our feelings, our joys, our situations, our frustrations, and our hopes as parents. Being a parent for the first time is not always easy and not always how we planned it. But we can be assured that God is active and present with the child and the parents. God's love surrounds the family as they grow together.

■ Things to Do

→ Start an album for the child. Include photographs, stories, and other items for the child to see as he or she grows. Maintain the album with successive volumes for the different stages of growth and maturity.

→ Create your own announcements to send to friends and family.

→ Remember and celebrate the day the child came into the family. This is especially significant for children who are adopted since it is likely a different day than his or her birthday.

→ Take photographs of the hospital where the baby was born as well as pictures of the doctors and nurses who assisted. Take photographs of the child's first home, both exterior and interior, especially the child's room.

→ Keep a journal, recording your prayers for yourself, for your spouse, and for your child.

→ Let the church know about the birth of your child so that it is publicly recognized (for example, a rose on the altar or an announcement in the church service and the church newsletter).

→ Take a picture of your child, and post it on the bulletin board in your church nursery.

→ Let your Sunday school class or other support group know how the family and the baby are doing.

→ Ask your pastor for the names of other parents who can provide support and encouragement to you, and answer your questions. Seek out experienced parents in your church and your community who share a similar home situation as your own.

■ Things to Talk About

→ What feelings do you have as new parents?

→ What changes will you need to make in your family and home—physical, financial, schedules, and so forth?

→ How will relationships with your spouse and others change?

→ Are there priorities in your life that need to be reevaluated?

■ For More Help

→ *What to Expect: The First Year* by Eisenberg, Murkoff, and Hathaway. New York: Workman Pub., 1996.

→ *What to Expect: The Toddler Years* by Eisenberg, Murkoff, and Hathaway. New York: Workman Pub., 1996.

→ *Your Baby and Child* by Penelope Leach. New York: Alfred A. Knopf, 1989.

→ *Infants and Mothers* by T. Berry Brazelton, MD. New York: Dell Pub., 1983.

- → *Your Child's Self-Esteem* by Dorothy Briggs. New York: Doubleday & Co., 1975.
- → *The First 12 Months of Life* by The Princeton Center for Infancy, Early Childhood. Bantam Books, 1995.

■ Devotional Moments

Scripture
Luke 1:57-58; Psalm 127:3

Song
"Our Parent, by Whose Name" (*United Methodist Hymnal*, No. 447)

Stories to Grow On

Sarah is our first child, and she loves to hear stories about her birth. Even though we moved from east Tennessee to the midstate area when she was only four months old, Sarah knows a lot about her birth from the stories her mother and I have shared. She also has shown great interest in seeing the places where she spent her first weeks of life.

When our family moved back to east Tennessee after thirteen years, Sarah, a teenager by this time, wanted to see the hospital where she was born, her first home, and the church where she was baptized. As Sue and I showed her these places and told her stories about her early life, I realized just how important these are for children.

Our daughter is mentally collecting stories about people and places and feelings that help shape her identity. She's heard about our feelings as we drove to the hospital in the middle of the night on the day of her birth; she's seen photographs of her grandparents after she came home. To this day as we ride by the hospital on our way to the mountains, she says, "That's where I was born."

Sharing stories about a child's arrival into the family is very important to the parents and to the child. By doing this, we communicate our humanity, our beliefs, and our identities to the generations to come.

Prayer
We give you thanks for this new baby. Please bless and watch over this child and over me as a parent. Help me to care for and nurture this child in all that I do. Amen.

2■Baptism

Baptism is sometimes referred to as the sacrament of belonging. Through baptism we recognize an individual as a member of the family of God. We are not baptized into a particular denomination but into the church of Jesus Christ. Baptism acknowledges God's claim on our lives and incorporates us into the community of faith. Although we may break the baptismal covenant, God's action is eternal. Therefore, while we may renew and recommit to the baptismal covenant at many points in our lives, we are baptized only once.

Because the love of God extends to people of all ages, United Methodists and many other denominations believe that children as well as adults are appropriate candidates for baptism. Whenever a person is baptized the entire congregation assumes a shared responsibility for nurturing the faith of the new brother or sister in Christ.

Once parents welcome a child into their family, they will be parents for the rest of their lives. When a child learns to read, he or she will retain this skill for a lifetime. Once a person learns to ride a bike or drive a car, these skills will always be available, whether or not the person makes regular use of them. Baptism is one of those moments in your life after which you will never be the same. Through baptism, the public recognition and acknowledgment of the presence of God's love through Jesus Christ in a person's life changes that life forever. Through Christian baptism a person is forever enfolded into the Christian faith. Even though we may forget our faith and stray away from Christian discipleship, God never forgets us.

■ From Our Faith Roots

One of the reasons that baptism has always been considered a sacrament by the church is because it is something that Jesus did and something he commanded us to do as well. In Mark 1:9 we read, "In those days Jesus came from Nazareth of Galilee and was baptized by

John in the Jordan." Then in Matthew 28:19 Jesus says, "Go therefore and make disciples of all nations, baptizing them in the name of the Father and of the Son and of the Holy Spirit, and teaching them to obey everything that I have commanded you."

Jesus' baptism was an outward public act that symbolized an inward recognition of God's claim on his life. Similarly, we are declared members of the family of God and called to live as children of God as part of our baptism. The service of baptism is not a time to "show off" a new child. For the congregation and the parents or sponsors, it is a renewing of the covenant between God and the faith community. For the individual being baptized, it begins the lifelong journey of discipleship and becomes a means of experiencing God's grace.

After his baptism Jesus began his public ministry. Through baptism every Christian is called to ministry. Whenever we are present at a service of baptism, we reaffirm our calling.

The water used in baptism is rich in symbolism. In creation God moved over and brought living creatures from the waters (Genesis 1:1-10 and 20-21). In Genesis 6-9 God used the waters of the flood to destroy sin. Water has symbolized both death and new life. There are three different methods that can be used in baptism: sprinkling, pouring, and immersion. Sprinkling reminds us of cleansing; pouring symbolizes the outpouring of the Holy Spirit; and immersion represents dying to sin and rising to new life in Christ.

It is not so important that we remember the service of baptism as it is the fact that *we are baptized*. When we remember our baptism, we remember who we are—beloved children of God called to live as faithful disciples of Jesus Christ.

■ Things to Do

→ Invite family members and friends to the service of baptism.

→ Take pictures of the people involved in the baptismal service. Create a photo album of the event.

→ Have a special meal and gathering to celebrate the baptism.

→ On the anniversary of the baptism, remember the event in some special way. If the church gave the family a baptismal candle, light the candle and have a prayer and a time of remembering.

→ Save objects (certificates, worship bulletins, clothing, and so forth) that help a person remember his or her baptism. Use the objects to help tell the story of the person's baptismal day.

Ask members of the congregation and family members to write a letter to the person being baptized, welcoming him or her to God's family. If the person being baptized is an infant, save the letters so they can be read to the child as he or she gets older.

→ Talk with your pastor about the meaning of baptism.

→ If you are in a Sunday school class or other small group, suggest that the group do a short-term study on baptism.

→ Find out when and where you were baptized.

■ Things to Talk About

→ What does baptism mean to me?

→ What does my church believe about baptism?

→ What difference will it make to have my child baptized?

→ How am I living out my baptismal covenant?

→ What will I tell my child about his or her baptism?

→ What changes do I need to make in my life in response to my baptism or that of my child's?

■ For More Help

→ *When Your Child Is Baptized* by Ron DelBane with Mary and Herb Montgomery. Nashville: Upper Room Books, 1991.

→ *By Water and the Spirit: Making Connections for Identity and Ministry* by Gayle Felton. Nashville: Discipleship Resources, 1997.

→ *Hand in Hand: Growing Spiritually with Our Children* by Sue Downing. Nashville: Discipleship Resources, 1998.

■ Devotional Moments

Scripture
Mark 1:9-11; Matthew 3:13-17

Songs
"Child of Blessing, Child of Promise"
(*United Methodist Hymnal*, No. 611)

A Child of God

Tim and Joan's new baby girl was eight months old. Amanda was a bright, healthy baby and a joy for her parents. Tim and Joan decided it was time to have Amanda baptized. They called their pastor, Reverend Walker, to make an appointment to talk about the meaning of baptism

14

and to make arrangements for the service. Reverend Walker helped Tim and Joan choose a date for Amanda's baptism. Since it would be a very important time for Amanda and the whole family, Tim and Joan invited the grandparents, other relatives, and friends to attend the service.

It was hectic getting everybody ready for the church service. Amanda wasn't in one of her best moods, so getting her dressed in the new outfit her grandmother had made wasn't easy. But everybody made it to the service on time and found their places in the reserved pew.

When it came time for the baptism, Amanda didn't want to go to the pastor, and she cried when the cold water was placed on her head. Afterward, Reverend Walker carried Amanda down the aisle of the church and presented her to the congregation. Reverend Walker reminded the congregation that not only Amanda's parents had taken a vow of responsibility but also each member of the church had made a similar promise. Amanda was now a part of the church family, and all members had committed to nurture Amanda in the Christian faith. Reverend Walker faced the congregation and said, "Today we recognize God's claim on Amanda's life. Baptism is a public event that initiates Amanda into the Christian faith and into a life of Christian nurture and discipleship."

Tim and Joan never forgot those words. Each time they see the baptismal candle in her room, they are reminded of God's love for Amanda and of the great gift entrusted to them by God. As Amanda grows, Tim and Joan will tell her about her baptism and show her the things that help them remember the important day when she was recognized, not only as their child but also as a child of God.

Prayer

Thank you God for the children you have entrusted to us, through birth and through baptism. I know that you have claimed me and them. Help us to live faithfully as baptized Christians so that others may also experience your love. Amen.

3 ▪ First-Time Events

Children experience first-time events throughout their lives. Who does not recall the excitement of the first solo bicycle ride, the anxiety of the first extended trip away from parents, or the anticipation of the first date? Significant "firsts" occur throughout our lifetimes, but a young child experiences these firsts at an unparallelled rate.

Children experience rapid growth in their first few years of life. Baby books are available for parents to record baby's first steps, first words, first solid foods, first Christmas, and first airplane ride. These events hold great importance for new parents. When a child is an infant, parents watch carefully for signs of new physical accomplishments. These events not only hold developmental significance for the child and emotional significance for the parents but also indicate transitions within the family.

Each first in the life of a young child brings renewed hope and excitement in the family. No parent wishes to be at work or out of town when the baby rolls over or sits on its own for the first time. Most parents would be very disappointed at missing their toddler's first unassisted steps or the appearance of the first tooth. Each milestone "first" is something never repeated in the life of the child. Other steps may be taken and other teeth appear, but nothing compares to the recognition of the firsts in your child's life. Significant "firsts" are indeed events to be celebrated and remembered.

▪ From Our Faith Roots

If we see God as a loving parent, we must believe that God has plans for families and for the growth and development of all children. In Bible times the family and religion were not viewed separately, as they sometimes are today. Biblical parents recognized and celebrated their child's growth as a gift from God.

Although many children are mentioned by name in the Bible, we do not have accounts of their significant early firsts. Parents in biblical times were probably just as thrilled with the major accomplishments in the lives of their children as parents are today. Imagine Mary happily watching the young Jesus toddle his way to Joseph, or Hannah listening with joy as young Samuel said his first word.

The Bible relates several events in the lives of children that were one-time occurrences and held great importance in the family and in their religious life. For male children the most significant of these was circumcision, which usually occurred eight days after birth. Naming of the child often accompanied this ritual act. (See Luke 1:59 and Luke 2:21.)

Another less known celebration for Hebrew parents was the time when a child was weaned from his mother, which usually occurred at two or three years of age. It signaled not only a physical independence from their mothers but also the time when young boys began receiving instruction about the Hebrew law from their fathers. Genesis 21:8 tells the short but beautiful story of this event in the life of young Isaac. We are told that Abraham made a great feast on that day and a celebration was held to commemorate this event in the life of his son.

■ Things to Do

→ Update baby books with memorabilia and photographs.

→ Make your own book (or videotape) of firsts, recording your child's significant events.

→ Mail updates to family and friends about your child's growth. If you have an Internet connection, consider creating a family website.

→ Suggest that your church use a nursery bulletin board to celebrate "big steps" in the lives of children. Display photographs and written accounts about the children's accomplishments.

→ Suggest that your church sponsor play groups and classes for parents of young children. Offer to help plan topics and activities for these groups, and encourage participants to support one another through prayer and attendance.

■ Things to Talk About

→ As a parent, how do you feel about the important events in your child's development?

→ How do you see your family life changing because of this event?

→ What preparations can you make to help the transitions in your family go more smoothly?

→ In what ways will this change affect your child? What can you do to make the adjustments easier for your child?

■ For More Help

→ *Family Fun* by Debbie Trafton O'Neal. Nashville: Dimensions for Living, 1995.

→ *One, Two, Three...The Toddler Years* by Irene Van der Zande. Santa Cruz, CA: Santa Cruz Toddler Center Press, 1995.

■ Devotional Moments

Scripture
Genesis 21:8; Luke 2:21

So Many Firsts

I couldn't wait until the day our daughter discovered her feet for the first time. Then I was eager to watch her try rolling over and sitting on her own. I can remember propping and surrounding her with pillows, as if this were all she needed to take the big step toward independence.

She sat unassisted soon enough, and before I knew it she was pulling up on the coffee table and taking her first steps. A few weeks later, the appearance of our house changed radically: The coffee table was cleared of all breakables, gates blocked the entrances to the stairs, all electrical outlets were sealed with baby-proof covers, and all cabinets were bolted with child-proof locks. Our baby was a toddler, and as a result our house was a fortress!

One night, exhausted from the day's adventures, I watched our child sleeping peacefully in her crib. Her first year of life had passed by so quickly! All of the accomplishments I had eagerly awaited had been achieved. If this year had gone by so quickly, the first day of kindergarten couldn't be far behind.

Watching children grow is a mixed bag of emotions for parents. We seem to want to accelerate the clock to see the new developments, but then we realize how quickly these pass. One day we are the cheerleaders for significant accomplishments, and the next day we are the voices of caution.

Whatever we do, nothing will stop our children from growing up. Like the parents of biblical times, we need to affirm our children's growth as a gift from God. Then, we become like the pillows we used to prop our children as they learned to sit alone: supportive enough to catch them if they fall but giving enough to let them develop at their own God-given pace.

A Parent's Prayer

My child is growing too fast.

Help me find joy in my child's new growth.

Help me, O Lord, not to be sad that yesterday is gone and that tomorrow is coming too quickly.

Give me patience as my child learns and discovers new abilities.

Help me nurture my child's eagerness and encourage attempts at new tasks.

Help me comfort my child's discouragement and ease the pain that comes with new frustrations.

Help me rejoice in my child's laughter and share in the tears.

Most of all, Lord, help me remember that growth is part of your plan for all children, even mine. Amen.

4▪School

The first day of school can be a stressful event for any student. Whether it is the first day of kindergarten, first grade, middle school, high school, college, trade school, or even military school, entering a new environment with new routines and new leaders can be overwhelming. Forging new relationships, accepting new responsibilities, and anticipating new adventures in learning may cause both excitement and dread among students and their parents.

On the other hand, one of the happiest, most carefree days for most students is when schools dismiss for the term or for the year. Regardless of academic performance, this annual event usually brings great relief to most students. Parents, however, meet the end of the school term with mixed emotions. Many are happy that the strict routine of the school schedule can be relaxed, but others dread the extended hours involved in planning activities for their children's leisure time. Some parents may also feel anxious about their children moving on to the next level.

Sandwiched between the beginning and the end of each school term are grading periods, or report cards. These may vary depending on the age of the child and the school system. For younger children periodic reports reflect mastery of certain fundamental skills, which can be easily celebrated. As a child matures, grades often reflect an ability to accept responsibility for his or her own work.

Most parents have high academic expectations for their children. If those expectations are not met through good grades, conflict often results. It is easy to praise our children for doing well. Accepting poor performance, finding new ways to challenge the student's abilities, and expressing disappointment without withholding love is not so simple. It is at these times that children need parental reassurance and redirection to help them maintain good self esteem.

School transitions are appropriate times to celebrate mental, physical, and social growth. Each new academic transition indicates an effort on the student's part, and such accomplishments call for celebration in the family.

■ From Our Faith Roots

Growth—mental, physical, social, and spiritual—is part of God's plan for each of us. The opportunity for an education is a gift many children today do not seem to appreciate, but it is something for which all children can learn to give thanks.

In Bible times education, like religion, was centered in the home. The mother was responsible for the earliest education of boys and girls through the age of three. Once the child was weaned from the mother, the primary burden of education shifted to the father for boys and continued with the mother for girls. It was at this young age that boys began receiving instruction in the Hebrew law. Fathers were also responsible for teaching their sons a trade. Jesus probably studied under Joseph to learn the trade of a carpenter (Matthew 13:55). Girls were instructed by their mothers in domestic duties.

The nature of education in Jesus' time was religion-centered and enabled students to understand the nature of God and what God required through the understanding of the Law. The synagogue school would become part of Jesus' education by the time he was six years old. Through repetition and memorization, boys were taught to read and write, among other things.

Other important educational experiences included the pilgrimages to the Temple in Jerusalem. The Scriptures say that Mary and Joseph went to Jerusalem every year for the festival of the Passover. During these religious celebrations, children and adults would hear the Scriptures read and have an opportunity to learn from the teachers. The only story the Scriptures record of Jesus' childhood is one that illustrates his desire to learn. We read that a twelve-year-old Jesus asked questions of the teachers in the Temple while his parents frantically searched for him (Luke 2:41-52).

■ Things to Do

→ Write a prayer for the beginning of each school year.
→ Make purchasing school supplies a family affair where everyone can help gather the materials for the new year.

→ Have a "retire-the-backpack" celebration at the end of the school year when supplies are put away until the next term.

→ Plan a special lunch for the first and last days of school.

→ For children going away to school, have a sending-forth celebration with family and friends. Shower the student with good wishes and blessings from loved ones.

→ Light a school candle at the dinner table at the outset and completion of each school year. Have a different candle for each child in the home.

→ Request prayers in worship for the beginning and the end of each school year. Pray for families, students, and teachers.

→ Ask Sunday school teachers to establish a "promotion connection" at the beginning of the school year so that they will know which children attend which school that year.

→ Suggest that your youth program connect students entering middle school or high school with other church friends who attend the same school. This can help ease student anxieties about the new school. The same could be done for new students in your city.

→ Ask your church's college ministry to stay in touch with students who are away at school. Provide correct names and addresses to members who wish to write the students.

→ Read with your child about starting school. (For younger children, read *Berenstain Bears Go Back to School* by Stan and Jan Berenstain; for older children, read *The Best School Year Ever* by Barbara Robinson.)

■ Things to Talk About

→ What are you looking forward to in your new grade (or school)?

→ What are your fears about your new class?

→ How do you think this grade (or school) will be different from your last?

→ Now that you are in (grade), what can we expect from you?

→ Name three ways that we (your family) can help you do your very best in class this year.

→ What was your favorite part of the school year that just ended?

■ For More Help

→ *Celebrating Families* by Lawrence and Diana Osborn. Nashville: Abingdon, 1995.

→ *Mr. Rogers Talks with Parents* by Fred Rogers. Milwaukee: Hal Leonard Corp., 1993.

■ Devotional Moments

Scripture
Luke 2:41-52

A Family Litany for the New School Year

(Before you begin, help your child list specific hopes, joys, and fears of the coming year. Insert your child's suggestions in place of the composed lines at the end of this prayer. Say the prayer together, with one or more people reading the leader's part.)

Leader: For a new year of school and new beginnings,
Response: We give you thanks, O God.
Leader: For new teachers who will help us learn and grow,
Response: We give you thanks, O God.
Leader: For our classrooms and our classmates,
Response: We give you thanks, O God.
Leader: For new backpacks, lunch boxes, and clothes,
Response: We give you thanks, O God.
Leader: For our family who loves and supports us,
Response: We give you thanks, O God.
Leader: (Write your own sentence here.)
Response: We give you thanks, O God.
Leader: (Write your own sentence here.)
Response: We give you thanks, O God.

Continue as needed to complete your prayer.

5■Pets

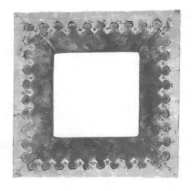

Having a pet is usually a child's first attempt at caring for another living creature and accepting the responsibilities, as well as the joys, that result.

Most pets are so endearing that they are thought of as members of the family. Losing a pet can produce a genuine sense of loss and trauma, particularly for a child. It is often a child's first experience with death.

Pets are totally dependent on their caregivers for the essentials of life, much as an infant is dependent on parents. All pets must be fed and their living area kept clean. Many require exercise and grooming. Each pet brings an added financial expense for the family, not just for food but for medical needs such as shots, spaying and neutering, and emergency care.

Caring for a pet provides children with wonderful opportunities for assuming responsibility within the family, provided the opportunities are not overwhelming for their age or unequally divided. Parents can help children adjust to the many needs of the pet and assist in setting a schedule for each family member to contribute in caring for the pet each day.

As the pet grows, its needs may change, providing children with different responsibilities. Some animals may grow too large for a family to keep. If that is the case, careful and early planning for how the pet will be cared for is essential to acting responsibly and with sensitivity.

■ From Our Faith Roots

The first chapter of Genesis tells the story about God's multi-faceted and wondrous creation. At the end of that chapter, we learn that God made people for specific purposes: "God blessed them, and God said to them, 'Be fruitful and multiply, and fill the earth and subdue it; and have dominion over the fish of the sea and over the birds of the air and over every living thing that moves upon the earth'" (Genesis 1:28). To have dominion over every living thing is an awesome task. This directive is a mandate for human beings to be good stewards of the earth and its creatures.

As we learn to be appropriate caretakers of animals, it adds to our appreciation for the world around us. God has fashioned some incredible creatures. Most pets ask no more from their owners than what it takes to keep them alive and functioning. Some studies show that people who have pets live happier and healthier lives. If this is true, then the responsibility that God gave humans in Genesis is not just for the good of animals but for the good of humans as well.

■ Things to Do

→ Use care when naming the pet. Think of a name that "fits," perhaps one from a biblical story mentioning a similar animal.

→ Take a photograph of your pet or draw a picture of your family welcoming the pet.

→ Send an announcement in the mail or through e-mail that informs friends and family about the new pet. A unique way of doing this is to send an announcement from the "pet," telling about his or her new home.

→ Keep a diary from the pet's viewpoint.

→ Work together to create a space for the pet, including a sleeping place and a meal place.

→ Establish a chart of responsibilities for each person who is expected to help with the pet's care. Post the chart where all family members can see it.

→ Ask your church if there are homebound members who would like a visit from your family and your pet. Be sure to consider allergies and appropriateness before you visit.

→ Ask your church's worship committee to plan a service of blessing for animals. A suggested service can be found on pages 608-610 of *The United Methodist Book of Worship.*

■ Things to Talk About

→ What will happen if we forget to care for our pet?

→ What should you be expected to do to help care for the pet?

→ What rules will we follow to make sure our pet is happy and safe?

→ The Bible teaches us to be responsible for animals and that God plans for us to care for animals. What do you think being a responsible caretaker means?

■ For More Help

→ *Peaceful Kingdom* by Stephanie Laland. Berkeley, CA: Conari Press, 1997.

→ *Pet Care Guide* by Lauren Scott and Robert Uherka. RJLA Press, 1997.

→ *Complete Book of Pet Care* by Peter Roach. New York: Howell Books, 1983.

■ Devotional Moments

Scripture
Genesis 1:24-31

Hymn
"All Things Bright and Beautiful"
(*United Methodist Hymnal*, No. 147)

Annie the Orphan

It was a day no one in our family will ever forget. As our daughters were leaving to go to a friend's house, they noticed the black dog curled up in the corner of our patio. She was a big dog, and she looked ill. From a distance I could see a cut on her nose and that her breathing was labored.

After sending the girls a safe distance away, I slowly approached the black furry creature. She lifted her head and stared at me with enormous brown eyes. I could see that she was injured, covered with fleas and ticks, and lacked identification, which led me to assume that she was lost or abandoned.

We gave the dog water and tried to clean her, but there were too many ticks to remove and too many fleas to spray. When we finally got her to her feet, she couldn't put her weight on her back leg.

All night we thought about what we should do. Take her to a shelter? Locate an owner in our neighborhood? Keep her? The latter option was by far the choice of our daughters! We had actually talked about getting a dog—a small dog, not one this big, and certainly not until our cat died.

When morning came, we put the dog in the car and took her to the vet. He kept her all day and overnight. When we picked her up the next morning, our girls heard the vet say the words they longed to hear, "If you ever wanted a family dog, this is the one to have." Despite all of her injuries, this poor, sad dog was loving and gentle; and once cleaned, she was beautiful!

Rick and I looked at the bill for the vet's services.

"Well," said Rick, "after spending this much on her, I guess she's ours." We loaded our new dog into the car and went home.

"What should we name her?" Sarah asked as she stroked the dog's head. We thought about that subject for most of the day. We finally decided on the name Annie because, like the comic strip character, she was an orphan looking for a home.

That was seven years ago. Since then we have learned that Annie is so afraid of thunder that she has to be sedated during a storm. We have also learned that she loves to chew on just about anything, including any type of paper and the seatbelts of my car. For all of these challenges, she is loved. Once when we thought she was lost, we were frantic; the moment we found her was full of rejoicing. We have nursed her through surgery, cleaned up accidents on the floor, laughed at her desire to chase (but never catch) squirrels in our yard. We rely on waking every morning to the thumping of her tail against the hallway wall. As much as any human that lives in our household, Annie is a member of the family.

Prayer

Thank you, God, for cats and dogs,
For hamsters, fish, and little green frogs.
For birds and turtles and, yes, for snakes too,
For all of our pets, God, we give thanks to you. Amen.

6 ■ Allowances

Money is a very important and powerful commodity in our culture. Money can bring about many wonderful things. It can also rule and control our lives. Responsible and wise use of money is an important lesson for children to learn. An allowance is a specific amount of money given to a child on a regular basis. Sometimes this money is given as compensation for the completion of certain household chores. At other times it is given to the child without expectations. The amount of allowance is usually determined by the age and maturity of the child, by the expectations and financial abilities of the parents, and by the needs of the child. There are no standards. Each family must thoughtfully establish an amount together.

Why give an allowance? An allowance is the first step in helping children learn about money and about being responsible for it. How to spend the money should be at the child's discretion, but he or she must be willing to face the consequences. Parents may give guidance and set ground rules for how an allowance is to be used; but as long as the child is living within those boundaries, he or she should be allowed to make the decisions about how the money is spent. This responsibility can increase the child's sense of independence and self-worth, and provides a way for children to improve their decision-making skills.

■ From Our Faith Roots

The Bible has many references to money but no specific verse about a child's allowance or about the amount to give children. However, parents will find guidance in advising children about how to use the money given to them.

The Bible is explicit about the love of money. In both 1 Timothy 6:10 and Hebrews 13:5, the writers warn against the love of money and the eagerness for wealth. Both can cause people to stray from the faith and the things that really matter. We should be satisfied with what God provides for our daily existence. In Matthew 6:24 Jesus warns that we cannot serve two masters. If our god is wealth, we cannot serve the one true God, and we will put one above the other. None of the biblical references claims that money is evil, or not good; instead, it warns us to be careful about our priorities. Where we place our love and faith is the most important thing.

The parable of the talents in Matthew 25:14-30 teaches about stewardship and about the use of money available to us, regardless of the amount. Immediately following in Matthew 25:31-45, Jesus reminds his disciples of their responsibilities in caring for those who are hungry, poor, and lonely. God wants us to use our money (talents) in good and resourceful ways. All are not given the same amount of resources in this world; but we are asked to use what we have in ways that can bring the greatest benefit to all.

Children learn much from their parents' behaviors and attitudes. The way parents view money, talk about money, and spend money will greatly influence their children. Make financial decisions that are in synch with your Christian faith, and your children will learn from your example.

Parents must teach children about the use of money in ways they can understand. Most families limit their expenditures according to their incomes. By discussing the wise use of money in everyday matters (entertainment, clothes, toys, savings, and so forth) in a way appropriate for the child, he or she will learn about making choices in today's world that are in accordance with their faith.

■ Things to Do

→ Have a designated family time to discuss the allowance: Why is it given? in what amount? in exchange for what? Are there guidelines for spending?

→ If saving is to be a part of the allowance plan, give your child a "piggy" bank or set up a savings account in the child's name at a local bank. Talk about the importance of saving and about what percentage should go into the account.

→ Help the child understand that giving to the church is a part of their allowance. Discuss the amount to be set aside for the church's offering in worship or in Sunday school. If possible, give your child his or her own set of offering envelopes.

→ Suggest to your child's Sunday school teacher that he or she explain how the congregation's offerings are used.

→ During your church's annual financial campaign, let your child make an individual pledge. Discuss the meaning of tithing.

→ When your child is old enough, help him or her establish a student checking account at a local bank.

→ When your child has managed to save for a big purchase, plan a special trip to the store. Celebrate the achievement with a meal.

→ Before going on a vacation, decide which expenses (souvenirs, snacks, and so forth) individuals will be responsible for and which expenses will be covered by the family budget.

■ Things to Talk About

→ How much allowance should you receive each week or each month?

→ Should you be expected to do certain household chores in return for your allowance? Why or why not?

→ How much should you save out of your allowance?

→ When should parents have input on the way you spend your allowance?

→ What are the "rules" for spending an allowance?

→ How does our Christian faith influence the way we spend our family income? How does it influence the way you spend your allowance?

→ Why do we give to the church?

→ How and when do we have a family discussion about a change in your allowance?

→ As parents, how do we model the value of money in our family, especially in light of our Christian faith?

■ For More Help

→ *Kids & Money* by Michael J. Searls. Summit Financial Products, Inc., 1996.

■ Devotional Moments

Scripture
Hebrews 13:5; Matthew 6:19

How Will It End?

Thirteen-year-old Brian and nine-year-old Stephen are brothers. Both boys had been given an allowance for a couple of years. Brian received a larger allowance each week since he was older and had more chores to do around the house.

Stephen was not used to saving his money. He didn't let money "burn a hole in his pocket" for long. Stephen liked the idea of having money to spend and didn't think much about how he spent it. Stephen also frequently complained to his parents about Brian receiving more money. Sometimes Brian had to give or loan money to Stephen when they went shopping.

Allowances became a constant source of irritation between the boys. They were always arguing about the amount of money each received and the stuff each purchased. Sometimes Brian complained that he had to work harder for his allowance. He liked receiving the larger allowance, but he thought the chores were unfairly divided.

One day Stephen asked his parents for an increase in his allowance. He had recently turned ten years old, and he thought he should receive more. Brian complained to their parents about Stephen's comparatively few chores and his indiscriminate spending. Brian also mentioned that his brother frequently asked to borrow money, and he didn't pay it back.

Eventually, the issue of the allowances became a serious source of conflict between the boys. Whenever the parents discussed it, Stephen and Brian lapsed into a "verbal war." The parents decided that the issue had to be resolved in a way agreeable to all. One night after dinner, the family went into the den for discussion. What do you think they said to Brian and Stephen? How do you think the story ended for the boys? What's the most important issue in this story?

Prayer
We give you thanks for all the blessings of life. Make us good stewards of all that you have given us. Amen.

7 ■ Puberty

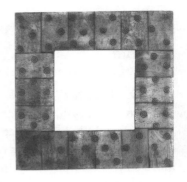

Puberty and the transition from childhood to adolescence is a very important time. During puberty, physical changes often occur at a faster rate than the mental maturity that brings an understanding of the changes. Moods and desires can change from one minute to the next. It is a time when a child can be taught the meanings of privilege and responsibility. But parents must be patient.

Sex becomes an issue as children mature physically. Decisions about how to be responsible for this "new" sexual body are of great importance. With the physical capacity for reproduction and the awakening of sexual urges, adolescent children must be informed of all aspects of reproduction and must be guided in developing Christian values related to the use of their bodies. Whenever children ask questions about the changes and feelings they are experiencing, parents must be honest, direct, and long-suffering.

Being a parent of a child going through puberty is not easy. While there are many good resources on the subject available, there are not easy answers to every situation. A parent must do the very best he or she can with the gifts, graces, and resources at hand to help a child deal with the changes of puberty. It takes time, patience, honesty, and a healthy sense of humor.

■ From Our Faith Roots

In 1 Samuel 1:1-19 we find the story of the boy Samuel. Because God had granted his parents a son in their latter years, Hannah and Elkanah dedicated Samuel to God.

While Samuel was still a young child, his parents took him to live with the priest Eli at the Temple and dedicated his life to God's work. The Bible says that Samuel grew in the presence of the Lord and continued to grow both in stature and in favor with the Lord and with men. When the appropriate time came and when Samuel was old enough to discern God's call in his life, God spoke to Samuel. Four times Samuel heard his name called. The first three times he thought the priest Eli was calling him. An obedient child, Samuel went to his teacher and asked why he was calling. Each time Eli told Samuel to return to his bed. Samuel did not yet understand that God was the one calling because "Now Samuel did not yet know the LORD, and the word of the LORD had not yet been revealed to him" (1 Samuel 3:7). The last time Samuel heard a voice call his name, he remained in his bed, thinking. Morning came, and Eli asked Samuel about what had happened during the night. At that point Samuel understood that the call did not come from Eli but from God. "So Samuel told (Eli) everything and hid nothing from him. Then he said, 'It is the LORD; let him do what seems good to him.' As Samuel grew up, the LORD was with him and let none of his words fall to the ground" (1 Samuel 3:18-19).

Through this story about Samuel, we see him first respond as an obedient child to his teacher and then respond as an adolescent with a greater understanding of God's call in his life and his role in that call. With God's call came greater responsibilities.

In Samuel we see many of the things that children and their parents go through at puberty and adolescence. Children question and desire independence, but they also want to please. They go through periods of change they do not quite understand. Then they begin to understand their roles in life. While Samuel lived a long time ago in a different land and culture, we can identify with some of the things he went through at this age. The constant is that God was there to guide and direct his journey into adulthood.

■ Things to Do

→ Create opportunities to discuss the changes that puberty brings and other issues important to your child. (For example, designate a "parent and child night out"—go to dinner and a movie or attend a sports event together.) Adolescents are often uncomfortable asking parents of the opposite gender about sex. Single parents may need to recruit trusted adult friends or relatives to spend time with their children and to answer their questions.

→ Recognize the rite of passage from childhood to adolescence with a special occasion or gift at age twelve, thirteen, or another time more appropriate for your family.

→ Allow your child to rearrange his or her room in a way that recognizes the new maturity. This could include painting the room a different color, selecting new furniture, changing pictures on the wall, and so forth.

→ Discuss the new family responsibilities that are to be expected.

→ Encourage your church to have a human sexuality study for older elementary or middle school youth.

■ Things to Talk About

→ If you could ask your mom or dad any question about puberty, without fear or embarrassment, what would it be?

→ Read (together or separately) and then discuss a selected book about human sexuality and reproduction.

→ Talk about how television and magazine advertisements portray sexuality.

→ Discuss what you wish to "put away as a child" and what new things you wish to "put on" as a teenager. (For example, being called Rick instead of Ricky.)

■ For More Help

→ *Reviving Ophelia* by Mary Pipher. New York: Putnam Publishers, 1994.

→ *Your Ten-to-Fourteen-Year-Old* by Louise Bates Ames. Delacorte Press, 1994.

→ *Parenting Your Teenager* by David Elkind. New York: Ballantine Books, 1994.

→ *Adolescence* by Elizabeth Fenwick and Tony Smith. London: Dorling Kindersley Publishers, 1996.

■ Devotional Moments

Scripture
Proverbs 3:1-8

Confusing Times

Margaret had about all she could handle as a single parent. Tim was fifteen and a freshmen in high school. Beth had just turned twelve and was going through puberty.

Beth and her mother had talked about sex before she started her first menstrual period. Beth thought her mother was being honest and giving correct information. But with an older brother who teased her about her changing body and all of the comments she heard at school, Beth wondered if she understood everything about the changes taking place. She wondered if her mother had really gotten all the information right.

One day Margaret overheard Beth talking to another girl about boys and sex. Margaret wanted Beth to understand the facts, but she didn't want to invade her privacy.

When they were alone the following weekend, Margaret had a chance to talk to Beth. In a caring and non-derogatory manner, Margaret explained that she had overheard Beth's conversation. Margaret said that she was often confused about sex when she was a teenager. During the conversation she told Beth the correct term for the slang word she had heard her use. Margaret offered to be available to discuss any of Beth's questions at any time. She promised to be honest about any subject. There were no lectures and little else said that night. However, Margaret felt that this one discussion had opened the communication links that would be helpful in the future.

That night Margaret prayed for strength, wisdom, and patience to survive the coming years of having two teenagers with differing needs and interests in the house. Through honest communication and the church's teachings, Margaret felt that her family could live and learn from each other through the years ahead.

Prayer
God, help us as parents to be loving and honest with our children during the years of change. Help us to know what to say and when to say it. Give us wisdom, patience, discipline, and love in all that we do. As you are the good parent to all of us, help us to be good parents to our children. Amen.

8 ■ Confirmation

As children grow, most decisions are made for them by the adults in their lives. There are also decisions and choices that children can make at appropriate stages of development. Infants are totally dependent on their parents for all life choices, but older children proudly select their own toys, clothing, and foods. As they approach adolescence, children begin making more crucial choices with more lasting consequences and responsibilities.

Confirmation is the time in a person's spiritual life when he or she makes a public profession of faith in Jesus Christ and declares an intent to lead a Christian life. When a child is baptized as an infant, the parent(s) promises to nurture the child in the Christian faith so that the child may be guided to accept God's grace and profess faith in Jesus Christ. When a child or youth has not been baptized prior to confirmation, the public profession of faith is made at the time of baptism.

The choice to live a Christian life is also one that individuals must make as they grow up. This decision may come as a sudden conversion experience or may be the conscious, guided decision that culminates years of growth as a nurtured believer.

Neither experience is more "real" than the other, and each signifies that the confirmand assumes responsibility for continued discipleship and growth in Jesus Christ.

■ From Our Faith Roots

God's love was with Jesus for all of his life. Mary, Jesus' mother, recognized God's love for her son. As Jesus grew, he became aware of this love. The Bible relates this emerging awareness of God's claim on his life in the story about Jesus' visit to the Temple. The twelve-year-old Jesus asked and answered questions of the teachers while his parents were looking for their lost child. When they found

Jesus he asked, "Why were you searching for me? Did you not know that I must be in my Father's house?" (Luke 2:49) It was at his baptism that Jesus fully confirmed and accepted his relationship with God as God's beloved son. This confirmation of Jesus' identity and purpose is recorded in the Gospels as the beginning of his public ministry.

Baptism is a public acknowledgment of God's prevenient grace in our lives. Baptism is our initiation into the family of God and the beginning of our spiritual journey. Confirmation is the recognition of God's justifying grace and another step in the individual's spiritual journey of accepting a life of Christian discipleship through works of piety (worship, Bible study, and prayer) and works of mercy (service and outreach to others, acts of justice and compassion, stewardship of time and resources). Just as Jesus' baptism and confirmation signalled the beginning of his public ministry, confirmation is a person's public acknowledgment of discipleship.

■ Things to Do

→ Make the entire day of confirmation a celebration. Invite family and friends to attend, and plan a special meal honoring the confirmand or have an informal gathering at home after the service. Make the day as important as a birthday or graduation.

→ Give a special gift. This may be the time to honor the newly accepted responsibilities of the youth with a significant gift, such as a new Bible, a watch, or other jewelry.

→ Invite your pastor to a family celebratory dinner the week after confirmation. Make certain you take a photograph of your child with the pastor.

→ Share family stories about confirmation and baptism.

→ Identify ways the family can work with the confirmand to carry out his or her new commitment to discipleship through worship, study, and service to others. Family outreach projects and Bible study are two suggestions.

→ Suggest that your church publish the names of confirmands in church bulletins or newsletters. If space allows, write a profile about each person.

→ Suggest that your church hold a banquet to honor those being confirmed.

➜ Suggest that your church give confirmands a special gift, such as a group photograph, a hymnal, or a Bible.

➜ Suggest that the adult classes pray for confirmands and send them notes of affirmation and encouragement.

➜ Suggest that your church offer specific ways confirmands can become involved in the life of the church, especially through service in choirs, as acolytes, as nursery volunteers, or through making a financial pledge.

▪ Things to Talk About

➜ Define the word "confirm." What does it mean to confirm an appointment or reservation? How is confirmation in the church similar?

➜ Why is confirmation important to you as an individual?

➜ What exactly does the church do? Give examples from your own experience.

➜ Why does your family belong to a particular denomination?

➜ What are the differences in beliefs among denominations?

➜ What responsibilities come with church membership?

➜ Identify ways you live as a disciple of Jesus Christ in your school or workplace.

▪ For More Help

➜ *Family the Forming Center: A Vision of the Role of Family in Spiritual Formation* by Marjorie J. Thompson. Nashville: Upper Room Books, 1997.

▪ Devotional Moments

Scripture
Mark 1:4-11; Matthew 4:18-20

A Different Confirmation

When Powell was less than twenty-four hours old, he suffered a massive stroke that left him severely brain damaged and with irreversible injuries to his heart and kidneys. From the day of his birth, Powell's parents knew that their son would not be able to participate in many of the activities considered important to their family, including active involvement in church.

As Powell grew older, it became obvious that he would not be able to communicate orally or with sign language. How then, when he reached the traditional age of confirmation in his church, could he make a public profession of his faith?

Powell was very fortunate. His parents, his pastor, and his church believe that God had a place for youth like Powell in the membership of the church. In 1992, the General Conference of The United Methodist Church passed legislation that allows people unable to speak for themselves to be confirmed as full members of the church. Powell was the first to be received under this new legislation, and in August 1992 his congregation took the vows of membership for him.

In spite of his mental and physical challenges, Powell has advanced much further than his doctors ever thought possible. He lives as a disciple of Jesus Christ among his peers at school and at church. He touches their lives with his presence. Powell's contributions will always be different from those of his peers. Simply by being who he is, however, he has made a lasting impression in his school and denomination. He isn't just the wheelchair-bound boy who can't talk; rather, he's one of God's children. He's a reminder of God's unconditional love, of inclusiveness in God's kingdom, and of the gift of God's grace, which transcends all things.

Prayer for Confirmation

We give thanks, O Lord, for *(name)*, who comes today to be recognized as one who chooses to be one of your disciples. Be with *(name)* each day, guiding decisions, and blessing *(name)* efforts to grow and understand your call in *(his/her)* life. Help us to be a supportive and loving family, and help us to grow together in service as your disciples. Amen.

9 ▪ Significant Accomplishments

Accomplishments can be defined as goals we set for ourselves and achieve throughout our lives. Significant accomplishments can be anything from making the football team to performing in a piano recital, from getting your driver's license to earning first honors in academics. Many accomplishments are momentary achievements. In twenty years, few people may care if a child made all A's in the third grade; however, for the third grader and his parents, it is an event to celebrate.

Families define significant accomplishments in different ways. In some competitive, sports-oriented families, playing a great game may not be as important as winning. To another family playing well and having fun are accomplishments to be enjoyed and remembered.

Conflict and misunderstanding can occur when family members disagree about what defines a significant accomplishment. Sometimes parents expect more than children are capable of doing. At other times children have unrealistic expectations of themselves. Both of these occurrences can lead to a loss of self-esteem.

If children do not perceive that they are valued by their parents, regardless of what they accomplish, they will suffer from poor self-esteem. When each person in the family is encouraged to do his or her best and those efforts are affirmed, children begin to believe that they are people of worth. Children also grow in confidence when they learn that success can be measured by genuine effort and a positive attitude.

▪ From Our Faith Roots

Everyone, at every age, needs to know that he or she is a valued child of God. In Genesis 1 we read that humankind was created in God's image. As we stop to consider what that means, we cannot help but feel that each of us is a valued creation!

1 Corinthians 12:4-6 speaks of God-given gifts of the Spirit: "Now there are varieties of gifts, but the same Spirit; and there are varieties of services, but the same Lord; and there are varieties of activities, but it is the same God who activates all of them in everyone."

Clearly, God has blessed each of us with gifts or talents to be used for God's glory. For most, it takes many attempts at many activities before we discover our true gifts and how to use them wisely. Any attempt approached with a positive attitude and an earnest effort is an accomplishment to be recognized and affirmed.

In the Bible, we discover many tales of heroic characters. What we can only imagine are the less dramatic accomplishments of everyday life that led an individual to become a person of faith who served God. David is certainly remembered for his defeat of Goliath (1 Samuel 17). Perhaps less recognized but just as important are the accomplishments of David the shepherd, who successfully protected his father's sheep from wild animals and who mastered the arts of music and poetry.

Each achievement recorded in the Bible or known to us today is preceded by smaller building blocks of accomplishments that shape us into a Christian community that serves God with each of our unique gifts.

■ Things to Do

➜ Schedule regular family conversation times. Encourage each person to name his or her accomplishment of the week. Affirm each person's choice. Encourage everyone to name things they recognize in other family members.

➜ Celebrate significant accomplishments with a special meal, either at home or at the celebrant's favorite restaurant.

➜ Begin a family scrapbook, consisting of mementos and photographs of the significant accomplishments of each member.

➜ Encourage your church to provide a way of celebrating important events in the lives of church members, such as reserving a parking space for the teenager who just received his or her driver's license or providing a centrally located bulletin board for posting announcements of special events in the lives of your congregation.

➜ Encourage your church to hold a "gifts and talents fair" where people of all ages can share their special talents, either through exhibits or a show.

➜ Have a daily family prayer to raise joys and concerns before God.

■ Things to Talk About
→ What do you do well?

→ Name ways that you can use your talents to serve God and the church.

→ How do you feel when you know you have done your very best at something? Do you feel just as good when doing your best means something less than winning first place?

→ What new responsibilities come with your most desired accomplishments?

→ How do you feel when a brother or sister receives special attention for accomplishing something you cannot do? How do you think your brother or sister feels when you are the one receiving the attention?

■ For More Help
→ *The Shelter of Each Other: Rebuilding Our Families* by Mary Pipher. New York: Putnam Pub., 1996.

→ *Starbright: Meditations for Children* by Maureen Garth. Harper SanFrancisco. 1991.

■ Devotional Moments
Scripture
1 Corinthians 12:4-7

I'm Not Sarah
When our younger daughter, Allison, entered public school, she was frequently compared to her big sister. Following in her sister's footsteps was an unwelcome challenge. Allison ended up in many of the same extracurricular activities as her sister: the same gymnastics classes, similar music lessons, and even the same Girl Scout troop.

Finally, when she was in third grade, Allison expressed her desire to try something nobody in our family had ever done before. "I'm not Sarah," she said frankly. "I want to do something that's only mine." So we sought an activity that only Allison could claim.

During the summer Allison enrolled in a pottery class at the local recreation center. She quickly fell in love with working the clay. As the summer progressed, she spent longer and longer hours in classes.

Allison learned more about a potter's wheel than anyone in our family, but her accomplishments weren't without trial and error. At first she lost more pieces on the wheel than she completed.

The first time I observed her hovering above a spinning pile of clay, I was astonished by the concentration I saw in her ten-year-old face and amazed at her intuitive feel for the mass taking shape beneath her fingers. I was proud of her creativity and her ability. Suddenly, after working diligently for a long time, the piece spun out of control and collapsed.

"I'm so sorry," I said in an effort to console her. As a mother who longed for her success, I was distraught that her efforts had failed.

"No problem," she said as she scraped away the clay. "That's the highest I've ever pulled the sides of a pot. It was great."

We created space in our home for every pot Allison made, regardless of its shape and color. We even had special cards printed for her to include in the pots she gave away as gifts. During the next school year Allison began private instruction. By the following spring, she had made enough pieces to have her own exhibit at a local crafts fair. The entire family pitched in to help, and Allison's first public art show became a treasured memory for us all.

From time to time she would humor the rest of us by trying to teach us her craft. Her sister and I both tried throwing a pot on the wheel, but we only ended up throwing our sad efforts away! We could never get the feel of the clay as Allison had. Her pottery is truly her own, and we continue to be grateful for her gift.

Today, thanks to her pottery, Allison has tried other forms of art and has even considered art as a major in college. Her search for being her own person and escaping from her sister's shadow not only gave our family many occasions to celebrate but also opened the door to many possibilities for a bright future.

Prayer

Creating and loving God, help us discover the gifts you have hidden within each of us. Help us strive to do our best in all we do, knowing that our best is all you ask of us each day. Amen.

10 ■ Graduation

Recognized as one of the great milestones in life, graduation is both an ending and a beginning. Graduation brings a sense of great accomplishment and a profound sense of the unknown. It opens the way for greater independence, but with that independence comes new responsibilities. The freedom most young graduates dream about when their formal schooling is over is quickly tempered by the realities of making it on their own in the world.

Everyone develops at different rates. All too frequently parents create a specific plan for their child's life, only to realize that their child has a totally different direction in mind. Parents should be aware of the many options available to graduates and encourage their children to explore them. In doing so, parents must first be willing to let their children take the major responsibility in mapping their own future.

Graduation not only means change from the school routine but also change in other areas of a person's life. Churches frequently group students according to the traditions of the community or culture. When youth graduate from high school, they are often moved from the youth department of their church to the college or career classes. In many African-American churches, young people remain with their youth programs throughout the college years. In some Spanish-speaking churches, people may continue attending youth activities until the age of twenty-five. Culture and tradition play important parts in the lives of graduates and should be considered as post-graduation plans are made.

For parents, graduation can be the ultimate time of letting go of their most precious "possession" and may trigger strong and sad emotions. It is important to remember that although the word *graduation* connotes an ending, the word *commencement* signifies a beginning. Discussing feelings about graduation can be meaningful to both parents and child. Working together with patience and love, families can celebrate this important life transition with joy.

■ From Our Faith Roots

Although formal educational opportunities are seldom mentioned in the Bible, we do have many stories that parallel the feelings of a graduate as he or she embarks in a new chapter of life, as well as many verses that instruct youth in ways they should live and conduct themselves as they approach adulthood. A large part of the Book of Proverbs is written for the instruction of youth. Proverbs not only offers instructions but also reminds youth to remember the guidance of their parents.

Jesus prepared his disciples for their ministry in much the same way as we prepare our children for graduation. He instructed them in God's laws as well as in ways they should treat one another. Jesus nurtured the disciples, he loved and cared for them, and he even gave them opportunities to be on their own for short periods of time to learn what it was like to witness and teach (Matthew 10:5-42). The disciples' "graduation" came with the empowering of the Holy Spirit at Pentecost, when they at last found voice and action for all that Jesus had prepared them to do. Their success depended on several factors: how well they had been taught, how deep their faith in God truly was, and how strong and confident they were in God's plan for their lives. Christian parents everywhere hope they have adequately prepared their children with the same tools as graduation day approaches.

■ Things to Do

→ Encourage your church to set aside time to honor graduating seniors with a special banquet or dinner.

→ Suggest that your church create a video or slide show that chronicles the lives of graduates in church activities.

→ Collect letters to the graduates from family and friends.

→ Plan a celebration for the graduate. Invite people of all ages who have influenced or touched the graduate's life.

→ Find out if the senior yearbook offers advertising space for sale to the parents of graduates. Many schools invite parents to take out congratulatory ads for their senior students.

→ Encourage your church to recognize graduates in worship. Consider letting them assume leadership roles in the service.

→ Remember how your graduate has grown and matured through the years. Chronicle that through a memory photo album or a framed print, or arrange photos on a hanging wreath.

■ Things to Talk About

→ What does graduation mean to each family member?

→ How was graduation different (and similar) for your parents and grandparents?

→ What has been your favorite year(s) of school? least favorite?

→ Who has influenced you the most in your academic career?

→ If you could re-live your school years what would you change?

→ How is graduation a beginning for you?

■ For More Help

→ *Leaving Home* by Herbert Anderson and Kenneth R. Mitchell. Louisville, KY: Westminster/John Knox Press, 1993.

→ *Goodbye High School, Hello College* by William H. Willimon. Dimensions for Living, 1992.

■ Devotional Moments

Scripture
Hebrews 12:1

Sent Forth in Love

When our oldest daughter was approaching her high school graduation, we found our entire family riding a rollercoaster of emotions. For her father and me, it was a time for reflection on where the last eighteen years had gone and for questioning if we had adequately prepared her for the years that lay ahead. Her younger sister felt ignored and neglected since Sarah's activities attracted so much attention. Regardless of our own feelings, however, we all wanted graduation to be one of the most special times in Sarah's life.

It was clear to us that many planned graduation events were not Sarah's first choice of things to do. Weeks before the events began, she predicted that baccalaureate would be a boring necessity. She viewed the invitation to speak in church on Senior Sunday as an honor but also a stressful part of her last week in school. Exams followed, as well as endless rehearsals. It was clear that we all needed time to have fun and relax. We decided to throw her a graduation party. Sarah made up the guest list, and the invitation insisted that "fun is mandatory!"

We let Sarah plan the food for the party and have final approval of decorations. Her sister gladly managed the decorations, which gave her an important role to play in the festivities.

Sarah's guest list was most unusual. She had included about thirty people, ranging in age from two years to sixty-five years. Included were family from out of state, friends from the city where she had spent her childhood, her closest youth friends from church, and a few friends from school. What made the party so unique and special was the inclusion of her friends' parents, people who had opened their homes to her through the years; the presence of pastors and youth workers who had been mentors in her spiritual journey; and the inclusion of the children (and their parents) for whom she had spent countless hours babysitting. Everyone had a wonderful time, but Sarah had the best time of all. Almost everyone she invited attended. Several who couldn't come took the time to call during the party to congratulate her, while others sent cards and flowers.

As I watched Sarah carrying a toddler, hugging an adult, and laughing with her peers, I thought about these special people and about the important place they hold in Sarah's life and heart. They were there to surround her with their love and support at one of the most important moments in her life. In his or her own unique way, each person had helped make Sarah the young woman she had become. Together in celebration on this special day, we gathered to send her forward on her life's journey with love, strength, and courage. There could be no more appropriate conclusion to one chapter of her life and no greater hope for the new beginning that lay ahead.

Prayer

> For endings that bring new beginnings,
> We give you thanks, O God.
> For beginnings that bring new challenges,
> We give you thanks, O God.
> For challenges that require newfound courage,
> We give you thanks, O God.
> For courage that we gain from our families who love us,
> We give you thanks, O God.
> For our families who give us roots to grow and wings to fly,
> We give you thanks, O God. Amen.

11 ▪ Milestone Birthdays

Culture and family environments are very influential in determining the significant birthdays of childhood, adolescence, and adulthood. One age may be considered important in a particular area of the world or in particular families. Religious or faith communities recognize reaching certain ages through rites and celebrations.

Western culture recognizes and celebrates its own milestone birthdays. The first birthday is usually celebrated with great festivity. The sixth birthday is sometimes considered a milestone because it signifies reaching school age. For some, thirteen is an important age since it signals the transition from childhood to adolescence. In the Hispanic culture the fifteenth birthday marks when a girl "enters" society and takes her first steps toward adulthood. The sixteenth birthday is usually associated with getting a driver's license. (In fact, getting the license sometimes overshadows the birthday.) Some teenagers look for part-time jobs after the sixteenth birthday. Getting a part-time job symbolizes some of the same things that are associated with getting a driver's license. It involves responsibility, some financial independence, and leaving the "nest" to move into the workplace.

Reaching the ages of eighteen, twenty-one, thirty, forty, fifty are meaningful markers in a person's life. Reaching retirement age can be celebrated or dreaded, depending on a person's outlook. The ages of ninety or one hundred can be times of thanksgiving for life or times of depression for lost independence or diminished health.

Milestone birthdays take place throughout our lives. It is important to recognize them, celebrate them, and let them give meaning to our lives. Whatever milestone ages you choose to observe, all are significant and provide "marking posts" in our life journey.

■ From Our Faith Roots

The Bible does not contain many references to birthdays, but it frequently mentions the ages of people at historic points in their lives. In the Old Testament we have several examples. The Bible lists Abraham's age at the time of his departure from Haran. He was one hundred years old when Issac was born. Issac was sixty when Jacob and Esau were born. Moses was one hundred and twenty years old when he died in the land of Moab.

In the New Testament accounts, ages and events are often connected. Luke 2:21 tells us that Jesus was circumcised and named when he was eight days old, as was required by Jewish tradition. Later in the same chapter we read that Mary and Joseph took Jesus to the Temple to present him to the Lord. While there, the prophet Anna, an eighty-four-year-old woman, praised God for the child. The Scriptures also tell us that Jesus was twelve years old when he accompanied his parents to Jerusalem to celebrate the Passover.

While accounts of specific birthdays are infrequent in the Scriptures, there is a direct correlation between significant events in a person's life and the age of the person at the event.

■ Things to Do

→ Always plan a significant and special way to recognize and celebrate milestone birthdays with family members. The ages and celebrations may vary from culture to culture and family to family.

→ Take photographs of the birthday person at the celebration.

→ Give a gift to the church or a charity in honor of the person celebrating the birthday. Possible suggestions include placing flowers on the altar, donating a book to the church library, giving a financial gift to a project important to the person, and so forth.

→ Encourage your local church to find ways to recognize the events in the lives of its members. Possible suggestions include announcements in newsletters and at church events, prayers of blessing and thanksgiving during worship, and so forth.

→ Print the birthdays of members (exclude the year) in the church newsletter so others can help celebrate.

→ Organize a group from the congregation to send notes of congratulations to members celebrating milestone birthdays.

■ Things to Talk About

→ What are the milestone birthdays in our family? What makes these birthdays different from others?

→ What new privileges and responsibilities come with our family's milestone birthdays?

→ How do you feel about reaching a milestone birthday? How does my culture and my family recognize these?

→ Are you looking forward to a particular birthday?

→ Which milestone birthdays make you anxious?

→ How would you like to celebrate your milestone birthdays? Have you shared those wishes with family members?

■ For More Help

→ *Family Celebrations at Birthdays and for Vacations and Other Holidays* by Ann Hibbard. Baker Books, 1996.

■ Devotional Moments

Scripture
Ecclesiastes 3:1

Leaving Home

When I was twenty-one years old, I left home—both literally and figuratively. In the fall of 1971, I took my first plane ride to Nashville, Tennessee, a city I had never visited, to attend Scarritt College, a place I had never seen. It was the first time I had really been on my own and away from home for a long period of time. Upon reflection, that year and age were significant for me as I "cut the apron strings," left the city I had called home, and developed a new way of living and learning on my own.

The year of my twenty-first birthday was one of celebration, anxiety, and excitement. I remember wrecking my car and having to sell it. Once I overcame that trauma, I happily realized that the money I received from the sale of my car enabled me to pay a greater part of my college expenses, enabling further independence. While I was excited about leaving home, I was quite anxious about going to an unfamiliar place. Still, in my private moments, I celebrated my new-found independence from daily parental "rule."

Even though my parents were concerned about their only son leaving for college, they helped me remember and celebrate the occasion. I received new luggage as a gift, and that made my first plane trip even more special. In addition, I sensed a new trust and confidence in our relationship.

After that first trip to Tennessee, I never really went back home. Oh, I visited Mom and Dad during holidays, summer breaks, and the time before my wedding, but Columbia, South Carolina, no longer monopolized my heart and mind. At twenty-one, I left home and found myself as I embarked upon an education adventure. Ultimately, I found a career and a wife. You can say that I left one home that year to begin the foundation of the one I now have.

Prayer

We give thanks for all that has happened before this time and all that will happen in the future. Help us to remember this milestone event and all that it means to our lives. Guide and direct us in the years ahead, and may we live as faithful disciples of Jesus Christ. Amen.

12 ■ The First Job

There is something indescribable about a first job. You never forget it, and you usually refer to it whenever you describe your life.

Some teenagers get their first part-time jobs during the high school years. It could be working in a retail store, working in a fast-food restaurant, or babysitting neighborhood children. Sometimes the first job comes after graduation from high school or college.

The first job signifies a readiness to accept self reliance. It affirms self-worth since it shows that another person or a company believes in your capabilities. It acknowledges your place in society as a person who can contribute. It creates opportunities to work with other people in new environments. The workplace is a "laboratory" for learning how to relate to and get along with people of different ideas, backgrounds, and ways of living. Long-term career choices are often influenced by the first job. People learn about work ethics, good and bad work practices, and how to treat other people in the world.

A first job is usually initiated by the need or desire for money. Part-time jobs allow teenagers to earn spending money, money to help with the family finances, or money to save for college. Whatever the case, the first paycheck is a very significant occasion in a teenager's life.

In a first full-time job, the salary is usually greater. With this comes more responsibilities and decisions about matters such as housing, food, clothing, insurance, and so forth.

■ From Our Faith Roots

In biblical times the first job for most people was helping in the "family business." Jesus' first and only job (before beginning his public ministry) was most likely that of a carpenter, which was

Joseph's trade. David was a shepherd of his father's sheep. James and John joined their father as fishermen.

A job can tell a lot about people, including their interests and values. Biblical writers considered it important for us to know that Zacchaeus was a tax collector; Peter, a fisherman; Lydia, a business-woman; and Priscilla and Aquila, tent makers.

We work to earn money to support ourselves, to gain a better sense of self-worth through the affirmations we receive, and to contribute to the good of the community.

Work is a part of God's created order and a part of every culture in the world. Adam and Eve were placed in Eden to work and care for the garden. Work sustains us, shapes us, and gives us purpose in the world. It is a part of God's plan for humankind, "so that you may lead lives worthy of the Lord, fully pleasing to him, as you bear fruit in every good work and as you grow in the knowledge of God" (Colossians 1:10).

Our first job launches us into the world of work, a part of God's purpose for all of humankind.

■ Things to Do

→ Help the new jobholder open a first checking account and establish a personal budget.

→ If the job does not provide a uniform, go on a shopping trip to buy appropriate work clothes.

→ Encourage the jobholder to do something special with the first paycheck—something they have always wanted and can afford.

→ Inform friends about the job, and find a way to celebrate with them.

→ If the new job conflicts with church commitments (youth activities), let the appropriate people know and, together, try to work out a solution.

→ Post an announcement about a member's first job on a bulletin board in the youth area.

→ Ask for prayers of encouragement and support for the jobholder during worship or at other times when the church family is gathered.

■ Things to Talk About

→ What is the real reason I am taking this job? Is it just for the money, or is it something I might like to do?

→ How will this job affect my family, my school work, my social life, my church life, and other personal commitments?

→ How will I use the money I make in this job?

→ What are the negative and positive aspects of this job?

→ Are there any sacrifices I will have to make for this job? If so, what are they?

■ For More Help

→ *First Job* by Richard Fein. John Wiley & Sons, Inc., Publishers, 1992.

→ *Get a Job You Love* by Roxanne S. Rogers. Dearborn Financial Publishing, Inc., 1995.

→ *What Color Is Your Parachute* by Richard Bolles. Ten Speed Press, 1997.

→ *Majoring in the Rest of Your Life* by Carol Carter. Farrar, Straus & Giroux, 1995.

→ *Creating You & Co.* by William Bridges. Addison-Wesley Publishers, 1997.

■ Devotional Moments

Scripture
Ruth 2:1-7; 1 Chronicles 28:20

My First Job

Even as I approach my late forties, I can still remember quite vividly the details of my first job at age sixteen. I took the job because my dad told me that if I wanted money for dates, for the latest clothes, and for other things, then I had better get a job.

It was scary applying for after-school, part-time work. I realized that my parents couldn't get the job for me; I was on my own. Most jobs available to teenage boys don't pay a lot of money or have a lot of prestige. This was certainly true for me.

My first job was at Roses Dime Store. I worked after school and on the weekends. The work was menial and sometimes very messy, and it required long hours. The undesirable tasks that nobody else wanted to do often came my way. Frequently I wished to be elsewhere and questioned why I even took the job.

However, my outlook about the job slightly changed once payday came. I opened my own checking account, saved some money, and spent some on whatever I wanted. It didn't change the tasks I did or how much money I earned, but it did change me.

My first job gave me a sense accomplishment for a task well done. It helped me learn to work with other people in the marketplace. It gave me a stronger sense of self-worth. It helped me learn how to manage my own money.

Throughout my high school and college years, I had other part-time jobs. Some were better than others. None had the same impact on me as that first job at Roses Dime Store. Upon reflection I know that God was with me in that experience. God was with me in my parents' support, guidance, and discipline. God's voice was heard in the kind and supportive words of an understanding employer, especially when times got rough. God's Spirit was with me as I learned to use the money I had earned. Even though I didn't know it at the time, God was with me during that first job, helping me to grow and to learn.

Prayer
God, be with me as I take this job. Support and guide me in my daily tasks. Help me listen to my co-workers and treat them justly. Never let me think too highly of myself, but grant me the wisdom to know when I am being treated unfairly. May all that I do and say in this job be to your glory. In Jesus Christ's name I pray. Amen.

13 ■ Marriage

Christian marriage is a sacred covenant between two people and God. It is a reflection of Christ's covenant with the church. It is a state that is to be entered into freely, yet with deep commitment and serious intent.

Marriage not only unites two people but also two families; in some cases it can unite two cultures. It frequently causes a few shifts in family traditions and the reestablishment of family values. It meshes the best that two families have to offer to create a new family unit. Such unions are never achieved without compromise, communication, patience, and understanding.

A wedding often symbolizes the romantic pinnacle of a relationship, but a marriage involves the nuts and bolts of day-to-day coexistence. Learning to live with another person's habits and idiosyncrasies is no easy task.

Most of us have heard (or experienced) the marriage tales of spouses who habitually forget to put the cap back on the toothpaste tube or who leave dirty socks in the middle of the floor. When the honeymoon is over and everyday living begins, many couples find that marriage is not what they planned.

In a society of quick fixes and instant gratification, many couples are unwilling to work through the realities that most enduring marriages face. The statistics are chilling: A high percentage of marriages today end in divorce; many married couples admit that marriage is harder than they thought it would be and question whether their marriage will last.

Being in love is the easy part. Fulfilling that love through the adjustments necessary to adapt to the daily lifestyle of another person is where the definition of love parallels the example of the enduring love of Jesus.

■ From Our Faith Roots

The most theological term associated with marriage is covenant. In the Bible, a covenant is a relationship entered into by God and the people. Jeremiah 31:33 states it best, "...I will be their God, and they shall be my people." The Ten Commandments were a symbol of the covenant between God and people.

In the written account of the Last Supper, Jesus speaks about the new covenant that would be sealed by his death. It is this new covenant that releases all believers from the power of sin to obey and worship God freely. In both instances the commitment within the covenant relationship is based on deep and abiding love and on an ongoing relationship that goes beyond the legalities of any simple agreement or contract.

The Bible is full of stories about marriages, and many of these reflect the customs of the times. Most marriages were arranged by parents. Although this might appear to overlook love, the feelings of the intended bride and groom were often considered when a match was made.

The marriage itself was preceded by a year's betrothal, a time when the relationship was as binding as the marriage itself. The betrothal could be broken only by legal means. It was during her betrothal to Joseph that Mary discovered that she was pregnant with Jesus. Under Jewish law Joseph could have brought charges against her, and Mary could have been stoned to death for violating the betrothal agreement. His great love for Mary and his enduring trust in God enabled Joseph to proceed with his marriage and fulfill God's plan.

Jesus' relationship with the church is often described in marital terms, and it is in these depictions that we find the blueprint for marriages that will last. In Ephesians 5 a husband's love for his wife is compared to Jesus' love for the church. To love the people of the church, regardless of their faults, frailties, and shortcomings, is to demonstrate the type of love and understanding necessary for marriage. Authentic love celebrates the good times but also endures the difficult ones with unfailing love and understanding.

■ Things to Do

➜ Celebrate the joys of marriage by telling your children about your life before their births. Talk about how your marriage has changed through the years. Show them your wedding pictures.

➜ Set aside a special private time to celebrate your anniversary.

→ Encourage your church to provide a service for married couples to renew their vows.

→ Invite other couples to an informal gathering. Ask them to bring their wedding pictures and tell their relationship stories.

→ Suggest that your church arrange a marriage enrichment seminar for couples.

→ Collect family wedding pictures from as many relatives and ancestors as possible. Show them at a family gathering.

→ Celebrate your marriage by planning "date nights" with your spouse. If childcare is a hindrance, set up a co-op with other couples, rotating the babysitting responsibilities.

→ Recognize anniversaries in your church bulletin.

■ Things to Talk About
→ How do you define "husband" and "wife"?

→ How do you feel about the option for wives to retain their maiden names?

→ Why do you feel that marriage is more important than living together?

→ What are your responsibilities toward your in-laws?

→ If you had to write a recipe for a successful marriage, how would it read?

■ For More Help
→ *Marriage Shock* by Dalma Heyn. New York: Dell Pub., 1998

→ *Staying Married and Loving It* by Patricia Allen. William Morrow, 1997.

→ *Becoming Married* by Herbert Anderson and Robert Cotton Fite. Louisville, KY: Westminster/John Knox, 1993.

→ *The Gift of Marriage* by Marion Stroud. Nashville: Upper Room Books, 1996.

→ *Couples Who Care* by Jane P. Ives. Nashville: Discipleship Resources, 1997.

→ *Marriage: Claiming God's Promises* by Jack Gilbert and Nancy Zoller. Nashville: Discipleship Resources, 1998.

→ *Growing in Faith, Communicating in Love* by Barb Nardi Kurtz. Nashville: Disicpleship Resources, 1998.

■ Devotional Moments

Scripture
1 John 4:7

After You Say, "I Do"

Melissa was twenty-one when she became engaged to Chris. Her family was happy about the marriage and gladly began planning the momentous occasion.

Three months before the wedding, Melissa's grandmother scheduled a dinner party for the young couple. Unlike other wedding parties, the guest list for this party was made up only by the grandmother.

When they arrived at the party, Melissa and Chris found a mixture of family, friends, and strangers. When everyone had gathered, Melissa's grandmother explained the nature of the party.

"These friends are couples with strong, lasting marriages. They know what happens after you say, 'I do.' They're here to share with you what they think makes a good marriage."

Melissa and Chris listened and learned. The advice was diverse: patience, a sense of humor, "choosing your battles," doing little things because you want to and not because you have to, arranging time to play and worship together, relying on God to give you all you need.

They also heard from couples who had faced serious illnesses and couples who had faced extreme poverty in their early years. Separations caused by military duty and work were also described.

Last to give their advice were Melissa's parents, who had been married for twenty-five years, and her grandparents, who had been married for forty-eight years. Each couple at the party wrote a letter to Melissa and Chris, and all of these were put in a memory book.

Melissa and Chris have been married for five years now. They still agree that the best advice they received before their marriage didn't come from books or counselors but from the guests who shared their "been there, done that" success stories.

Prayer

Loving God, who binds heart to heart and life to life, bless those we love who seek to enter marriage this year. Bless their union and strengthen them to always seek your will and seek good for their lives as individuals and their life as a couple. Amen.

14■Pregnancy

A pregnancy can bring joy or anguish to the people involved. There was a time when the logical order dictated that pregnancy was preceded by marriage. In today's society pregnancy often occurs outside of marriage, and a staggering number of teenagers are becoming parents. These facts help us realize that expecting a child is not always the joyful experience it once was.

Women facing an unexpected pregnancy may experience the birth of the child alone or with little support from the baby's father or from their own family. For these women, the child they carry may not seem to be a gift from God.

Pregnancy can make a woman feel out of control and that her body is no longer her own. She must be ever mindful of stimuli and environments that may affect her unborn child. The physical changes that accompany a pregnancy can cause great confusion and tension to everyone in the family. Even in the course of a normal, uncomplicated pregnancy, the hormonal changes, the mood swings, the fatigue, the discomfort, and the insomnia are enough to strain the best of relationships.

Parents-to-be also experience a great sense of anxiety during pregnancy. The health of the unborn child is a constant concern. Questions about being able to properly nurture the child and provide the necessities of life also arise. Such questions of adequacy and coping can be intensified if the pregnancy is unplanned.

Sadly, not all pregnancies result in the birth of a healthy child. A miscarriage can be as devastating as the death of a child that has been born. Parents who lose an unborn child must be allowed time to grieve, and they need the support of loving family and friends.

Creating a life and bringing it into the world is an awesome power and an equally awesome responsibility. Women are allowed the opportunity to bear children for only a portion of their lives. We must willingly assume our roles as parents when we accept the gift of the birth of a child. Embarking on the journey of parenthood requires patience, care, and a great deal of self education, as well as time for celebrating the wonderful gift of a child.

■ From Our Faith Roots

Reproduction is a natural part of our human sexuality. The ability to create a life is a sacred and wonderful trust from God. The early Hebrews believed that a man lived on through his children. Without children, there is no future.

In Bible times, having many children was considered a blessing from God. In these patriarchal times women were seen as being the property of their husbands. Indeed, one of the primary roles of the wife was to bear children. Women continued to work and care for the home during pregnancy. After the baby was born women were considered ritually unclean until proper sacrifices were made.

Although the Bible tells us little about the conditions of pregnancy, it is full of stories about women and men who prayed and waited for a child. Abraham and Sarah prayed for many years and were indeed very old before Isaac was conceived (Genesis 21:1-7). Rachel watched her sister bear Jacob many children before she gave birth to Joseph (Genesis 30). Hannah prayed for a son, promising to dedicate the life of the child to God if her prayer was answered (1 Samuel 1). Being able to bear a child was looked upon as being blessed by God. However, sons were favored over daughters.

Usually most homes were filled with joy when a pregnancy was made known. Probably the most familiar New Testament pregnancy story is that of Mary, who learned from the angel Gabriel that she was expecting a son. In Mary's case the circumstances were less than perfect: She was not yet married to Joseph, and as his betrothed wife, she was subject to expulsion and even death if she were found guilty of adultery.

We know the ending of the story. Joseph was also visited by the angel. He chose to care for Mary and her son and raise him as his earthly son. In Luke 1 we read Mary's song of praise at the prospect of having this special child. Her words are so full of elation and thankfulness that they could be the words of any mother-to-be who is looking forward to the birth of her child with joy and wonder.

■ Things to Do

→ Keep a journal of your pregnancy. Include your hopes and dreams for your child.

→ Learn more about your family tree and chart it for your child's baby book.

→ Ask your church to begin a support group for expectant parents; perhaps combine it with a Bible study.

→ Collect baby photos from your own childhood.

→ Talk with your parents about how they felt before you were born.

→ Ask your church to host a meeting for familiarizing expectant parents about what the church offers to infants and their families.

■ Things to Talk About

→ How do you feel about the titles "Mom" and "Dad"?

→ If both parents work outside the home, discuss the possibility of paternity leave versus maternity leave.

→ What do you think will be the most difficult adjustment to make as you are waiting for the baby to arrive?

→ How do you see your life changing for the better after the baby arrives?

→ How do you think this pregnancy would have been different if it were a surprise? planned?

■ For More Help

→ *Regarding Children* by Herbert Anderson and Susan B. Johnson. Louisville, KY: Westminster/John Knox Press, 1994.

→ *The Gift of a Child* by Marion Stroud. Nashville: Upper Room Books, 1996.

→ *Meditations for New Parents* by Gerald and Sara Wenger Shenk. Herald Press, 1996.

→ *The Pregnancy Book* by William Sears and Martha Sears. Little - Brown Publishing, 1997.

■ Devotional Moments

Scripture
Psalm 127:3

A Gift From God

Martha left the doctor's office with mixed emotions. Just a few hours earlier she had suspected that, at age thirty-nine, she was experiencing the symptoms of early menopause. Medical problems over the last eleven years had led her to believe that she would be unable to have another baby. Suddenly, all of that had changed. Martha was pregnant with her second child.

After putting their ten-year-old son David to bed that evening, Martha and her husband Richard tried to absorb the news of the impending birth. Their emotions were like rollercoasters. Laughter and joy were soon replaced with concerns about the anticipated changes to their lifestyles: starting over with diapers and night feedings, childproofing the house, taking time off from their jobs.

As their concerns mounted, the happiness about the new life resurfaced. Martha and Richard were soon smiling as they recalled David's infancy and the love he had brought into their home.

The next moment they wondered if they could love another child as much as they loved David. Would they be able to send two children to college? Could they actually convert the den into a nursery?

Then, again, the smiles came. Martha reached into the closet and pulled out David's baby book, something she hadn't looked at in years. From the pages fell a small verse that they had received from their church on the day of David's birth. She read aloud the verse from the Psalms, "Children are a gift from the Lord; they are a real blessing."

Martha and Richard had no more doubts. Their new baby was a gift from God, as all children were, but in this case a wonderful surprise.

Prayer

Thank you God for new life. Help us to remember that all life is a gift from you, and that this child is a gift to be cherished and nurtured. Amen.

15■Divorce

Even though divorce is more common today than it has ever been in the past, it is not any easier. Divorce is a traumatic and wrenching experience for all involved. It signals the end of the most significant relationship that a man and woman can have in our culture. It is the end of something deemed sacred. Regardless of the cause, divorce is a life-changing experience. Husband, wife, children, in-laws, friends, and others are affected by the physical, psychological, and social ramifications of a divorce. Even after the legal issues are resolved, the effects can linger for years.

Divorces happen for many reasons: physical or psychological abuse, adultery, traumatic life events, incompatibility, and so forth. Before a divorce ever becomes final, there are many factors that lead to the end of a marriage. Some couples recognize a problem at its outset and take steps to work it out. Some couples or individuals ignore the initial problem and behave as if nothing were wrong. The problem only becomes bigger and causes more friction in the marriage. Some people just want to get out of the marriage at any cost. Some couples have done all they can to address problems in their marriage, and still the relationship remains broken.

No matter how people view divorce through social, religious, and psychological lenses, it is a part of our society and needs to be dealt with in an honest, compassionate, reconciling, and grace-filled manner.

■ From Our Faith Roots

Marital faithfulness is the ideal promoted throughout the Bible. The prohibition of adultery is one of the Ten Commandments. The bond of marriage was considered synonymous with the bond between God and Israel. The married couple was to develop mutual trust, love, and respect, and thus, pass on this model to their children.

When divorce is mentioned in the Old Testament, it is only initiated by the husband through a letter delivered to his wife's hand. Even though divorce was legal, it was still viewed unfavorably by society, and it was very costly for the husband: He would have to return the dowry received from his wife's family and make large payments to his former wife.

In the Gospels, we find Jesus' opinion about divorce in Matthew 19:1-11 and Mark 10:2-12. In these passages Jesus is fairly clear about divorce. He disagrees with the Mosaic divorce law and uses Genesis 2:24 as a standard "the two shall become one flesh" and, thus, "what God has joined together, let no one separate."

The fact that Jesus was asked about divorce indicates that the practice did occur and was an issue for the church. Jesus takes a civil law and transcends it with God's ultimate will. God's will for married couples is that they love and respect one another. We have laws for divorce because, sadly enough, we often do not live in tune with God's will. Because we do not live as if the kingdom of God is here, we must have laws that guide us through divorce. Marriage, like life itself, is not always perfect. Continually, we have to seek reconciliation and move toward God's will for all of humankind. Families are hurt when divorce occurs, and God is hurt as well.

■ Things to Do

→ Recognize and affirm the different feelings you are having in the divorce process. It is okay to have these feelings.

→ Seek professional counseling from an accredited Christian counselor or one that is recommended by your pastor.

→ Plan a church-sponsored divorce recovery workshop.

→ Ask your church to sponsor a recovery program for children affected by divorce.

→ Stay connected to friends and a support group in your church.

→ Let close friends know about your needs. This could be the time that they can minister to you.

→ Network with others who have gone through a divorce and are coping with it in a healthy manner.

■ Things to Talk About

→ What steps do I need to take to get through this process? Be honest and realistic.

→ What changes will I need to make in my everyday life? What parts of my life will not be the same?

→ How will I help the children cope? What do I need to tell them?

→ To whom can I talk and ask for help when I need it?

→ How does my church feel about divorce? What support can I find at my church?

→ Where do I go to learn how to be single again?

■ For More Help

→ *The Fresh Start Divorce Recovery Workbook* by Bob Burns and Tom Whiteman. Nashville: Thomas Nelson, 1992.

→ *Divorce Book for Parents* by Vicki Lansky. Deephaven, MN: The Book Peddlers, 1996.

→ *Let's Talk About It: Divorce* by Fred Rogers. Philomel Books, 1996.

→ *Why Are We Getting a Divorce?* by Peter Mayle. Crown Pub., 1988.

→ *Starting Again: A Divorce Recovery Program* by Sandra Scott. Nashville: Discipleship Resources, 1997.

■ Devotional Moments

Scripture
Psalm 28:6-7

Starting Again

Jane and Tim had been married for more than seven years and had three beautiful children. They lived in a nice house, and everything appeared to be going well. From all outward appearances, they seemed to be the "model family."

Immediately after the Christmas holidays one year, the bombshell dropped. Tim announced that he wanted to divorce. Jane later found out that Tim was having an affair with another woman. Their world as a family began to fall apart.

Everything in Jane's life changed. She had to move out of the house and buy a condominium. She had to get a job and begin to support herself and the children. An adversarial relationship began to develop between Jane and Tim. The children were trapped in the middle.

The divorce process wasn't easy for Jane, Tim, or the children. Years were spent in the courts deciding "who would get what." The children needed professional help to deal with their feelings. There were battles for custody, child support, and alimony. A lot of money was spent on lawyers. The emotional scars were equally shared.

However, Jane and the children had the support of family, friends, and their church. As much as possible, Jane helped the children keep a routine and stay connected with people who loved and cared for them. Their lifestyles changed, things were sacrificed, and everyday living was hard. At times, Jane didn't know if she could go on.

Little by little, things did begin to improve. Life wasn't the same, but it was getting better. Jane was able to get on with her life. She found a better paying job and the family was able to buy a house. Her children began to vent their feelings in a positive way.

This isn't to say that everything is now wonderful. The children don't really enjoy the weekend visits with their father, and Jane questions whether she would be able to commit to a serious relationship again. There are still financial strains on the household budget.

Divorce wasn't easy for this family. Yet, through it all, Jane and the children have survived and grown in their coping skills. They have experienced the ongoing love of God through their extended family, close friends, and the church. God's love has always been there for them in the form of loving arms, a sympathetic ear, reassuring words, and strong unwavering support. Through all of the tears, questions, loneliness, and self-doubt, God has been and continues to be present.

Prayer

Loving God, give us strength, wisdom, and guidance through difficult times. Amen.

16 ▪ The Arrival of a Sibling

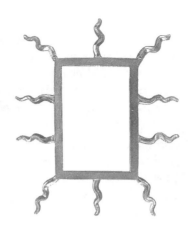

When another child arrives in a family, everything changes. Additional children mean a redistribution of the family belongings, time, and space. Parents may struggle with practical and economic issues. Is there enough space for another child? How will we support another child? What impact will the child have on our jobs?

Parents may also struggle with questions of adequacy similar to those felt during earlier pregnancies. Will we be able to cope with another child? Will we be able to divide our attention evenly among the children?

Children will have questions about how an addition to the family will affect them. Will Mom and Dad love the new baby more? Will I still get to do the things I do now? What will I have to give up because of my new brother or sister? Jealousy among siblings is common, and parents need to think carefully and plan ways to help older children minimize their jealousy. Based on their level of understanding, children need to feel that they are an important part of the planning for the new child. Children also need to know that there are ways they can help when the new child arrives. They must feel affirmed for their participation in the family transition.

Regardless of how many children are in a family, each member is a unique gift from God. Each brings something special and new to the home and should be welcomed and accepted by all for the gifts he or she brings.

▪ From Our Faith Roots

The Bible is full of stories about siblings. In Genesis the first sibling conflict (between Cain and Abel) is recorded. A similar account about the conflict between the twins Esau and Jacob appears later. Jacob was the father of twelve sons. Because Joseph was favored by Jacob, his older brothers conspired to fake his death. They eventually sold Joseph into slavery.

There are many lessons to be learned from these stories, not only about getting along with a brother or sister but about how parents view and treat their children. Certainly in Jacob's case, his open favoritism toward Joseph, the first son of his beloved Rachel, led to the intense rivalry among the brothers. As God intervened and used their evil act (not only for the survival of the family but also for the survival of a nation), the brothers learned that tolerance and acceptance were very important to their relationships.

From what we read in the Bible, Jesus seemed to be especially close to the family of Lazarus and his sisters, Mary and Martha. We have several accounts of their interaction as siblings in Luke's Gospel, but none indicates the differences in interests and personalities like the story in Luke 10:38-42.

As Jesus and his disciples visited with the family, Martha is stressed by her duties of making preparations for the guests—cooking, cleaning, and serving. Mary, however, does not bother to help. Instead she listens to Jesus, choosing to forego the expected duties of the women in favor of learning more about Jesus' message. Martha calls on Jesus to demand that Mary help her. She is no doubt surprised when Jesus actually affirms Mary's non-traditional choice. This story clearly shows the personality differences between the two sisters, yet Jesus loved them both.

In both the Old and New Testaments, we read about siblings who had problems that are similar to ours today. From these stories, we learn the lessons of God's continuing work in each person's life and the way family members can overcome obstacles and adversity through strong faith.

■ Things to Do
→ Let the older sibling(s) select a gift for the new baby and plan ways to help when the baby comes home.

→ Choose a gift from the new baby to give to the older child(ren).

→ Plan a "big brother" or "big sister" day, and celebrate what the older child(ren) can do.

→ Plan a welcoming party for the new child.

→ Give the older child(ren) a significant gift when the new sibling arrives, such as a new bed or a new toy.

→ Give the older child(ren) disposable cameras and put them in charge of photographing the new sibling.

→ Plan a special outing that takes the older child(ren) away from the new sibling. Go to a movie, to the library, or another special place.

→ Encourage your church to recognize the entire family, including siblings, when the birth or adoption is announced.

→ Encourage your church to have a "New Arrivals" bulletin board. Include the older siblings in a photograph with their new baby brother or sister.

→ Look at the baby books of the older children. Recall their growth and accomplishments.

■ Things to Talk About

→ What does the new baby do that you think is funny?

→ What does the new baby do that drives you crazy?

→ What are the ways you can help with your new brother or sister? Make a list.

→ How do you think the family will change because of this new member of the family?

→ What are the fun times we have had together as a family?

■ For More Help

→ *Your Second Child* by Joan Solomon Weiss. Summit Books, 1981.

→ *Siblings Without Rivalry* by Adele Faber. Avon Books, 1996.

→ *Celebrating Families* by Lawrence and Diana Osborn. Nashville: Abingdon, 1995.

→ *The Birth Order Book* by Kevin Leman. New York: Dell Books, 1992.

■ Devotional Moments

Scripture
Psalm 127:3

Sisters Forever

Our older daughter was twenty-eight-months old when her sister was born. As soon as it was evident that a new baby was on the way, we began including Sarah in the planning and preparation. As much as possible we included her in fixing the baby's room, choosing a name (although she preferred Sally or Bruce to Allison or Andrew), and deciding what she might do while we were at the hospital for the birth.

As it turned out, Allison was two weeks late. Sarah had her grandmother, who had come to help, all to herself for much of that time. Her grandmother told her stories about all of the babies she had known and how much fun they could be. She also told Sarah what a great sister she would be.

Two things that we had the presence of mind to do during that time really made a difference: We decided to let Sarah be the "voice" on the birth announcements, and we made certain that Allison had a gift for Sarah when she came to visit the hospital for the first time. The gift we selected was a small, not very cute, Mickey Mouse doll.

The tattered, sad Mickey Mouse remains on Sarah's bed today, even though Sarah is nineteen. It has not always been her favorite stuffed animal. In fact her favorite was an equally ugly bear named Montana. The bear was her constant companion until he was left overseas after a mission trip. I lamented the bear's demise, but Sarah really surprised me. "I can live without Montana as long as I have Mickey," she said. "If I lost him, I don't know what I'd do."

As our daughters have grown, we frequently have had to remind them of how important they'll always be to each other. They argue, they disagree, and they become frustrated with each other; but when everything else is put aside, the results are like Sarah and Mickey: Without the other, neither would be complete.

Prayer
Thank you God for brothers and sisters. Even when we argue or fight or disagree, help us to remember how important they are. Strengthen our bond, and help us always know that your love will guide us wherever we go. Amen.

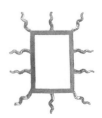

17 ■ Vacations

Vacations remove us from the work routines that consume most of our lives. No one can do the same thing day in and day out, for years at a time, and remain enthusiastic and creative. In taking time away from our daily routines, we can return to them refreshed, rested, and with a fresh perspective. Everyone deserves and needs a vacation, whether it is one away from school work, house work, or a job.

In today's society vacations can vary. Not everyone is able to take extended vacations. While some families have the time and resources to take long vacations to exotic locations, these are not essential elements for family fun and refreshment. With a little creative planning, a vacation can happen without leaving town or depleting the family finances. Mini-vacations can have a positive effect on a family's life together.

Whatever form it takes, a family vacation can help build traditions and memories. There is something very holy about families having fun together. Spending time together creates an opportunity for open and sustained communication, something that is often difficult during the business of our daily lives.

Regardless of where vacations are taken or of how long they last, the key to success is good planning. Parents, for example, must consider the ages and abilities of the children. A two-year-old may enjoy a few hours at a major theme park, but a twelve-hour car ride or a three-hour plane trip to get there may not be such a good idea. Vacations that overwhelm and exhaust family members do not provide the relaxation and renewal that is needed.

Vacation time should be balanced to include activities all family members enjoy and should include both active time as well as time to relax.

■ From Our Faith Roots

In Genesis 2:2-3 we are told that God rested on the seventh day from the task of Creation. If the need for rest is so important that even God required it, then our need for renewal should go without question.

Through the Creation story, Israel came to believe that the seventh day belonged to God. The celebration of the Sabbath became a weekly festival after six days of work. The Sabbath was set aside for rest. It was a day that people refrained from work, travel, or idle talk. The Sabbath was reserved for remembering what God had done in people's lives.

By the time of Jesus, the Sabbath had been complicated by rules and regulations. Jesus reminded his followers that the Sabbath was made for man and not man for the Sabbath (Matthew 12:1-14). The Sabbath was a day to rest, a day to remember, and a day to worship God.

Although we do not have accounts of Jesus taking vacations from his work, we do see the importance of "time apart" in his ministry. When the crowds began to weary him, Jesus would withdraw for a time of solitary prayer. Even Jesus recognized the importance of personal renewal so that his work would continue to be effective. Part of Jesus' renewal was prayer or reconnecting with God. In today's world we too often think solely in terms of physical renewal, not spiritual. It is important that our vacations "feed" our bodies, our minds, and our spirits.

■ Things to Do

→ Find places in your own community that you can visit inexpensively on a "home vacation." Consider local museums, parks, zoos, and places you have not visited for awhile.

→ Start each trip with a family prayer.

→ Visit a different church while on vacation.

→ Ask your church to create a vacation display so members can bring back bulletins from churches they have visited.

→ Look at family photos of previous vacations before planning your next one.

→ Plan to visit extended family on your vacation. Share stories of family history and traditions while you are together.

→ Encourage your church to offer renewal weekends (retreats or camps) for families.

→ Visit a local library, bookstore, or travel agent to obtain more information about the place you have chosen to visit. Let everyone take part in deciding the details for the trip.

■ Things to Talk About

→ What has been your most favorite family vacation?

→ What can we take to make the trip more pleasant while we travel?

→ What are some things we can do to make this vacation less expensive and more refreshing?

→ Establish ground rules for things you can and cannot do on vacation so that the time apart will be relaxing and fun for all.

→ What responsibilities will each family member take on to make the vacation more successful?

■ For More Help

→ *Outside Magazine's Guide to Family Vacations.* MacMillan Publishing, 1997.

→ *Super Family Vacations* by Martha Shirk and Nancy Klepper. New York: HarperPerennial, 1995.

→ *Family Fun* by Debbie Trafton O'Neal. Nashville: Dimensions for Living, 1995.

→ *Family Time: 101 Great Ideas for Sunday Afternoon* by Debbie Trafton O'Neal. Nashville: Dimensions for Living, 1994.

■ Devotional Moments

Scripture
Psalm 118:24

The Family's Vacation

The year their oldest child graduated from high school, Bob and Linda discussed what might be a memorable summer vacation for their family. After all, it could be the last year the entire family would vacation together.

They came up with several suggestions to offer their three children. One idea was a trip to New York City. Another suggestion was to drive across the country to camp for a week in a national park. The third suggestion was a week at one of Florida's largest theme parks. Sure that these would appeal to their children, they called a family meeting to make a final decision.

They presented their ideas and shared with their children the colorful brochures and maps for each suggestion.

"What about our trip to the beach?" Kelly asked. For the past ten years the family had spent a week at the same beach with their grandmother, aunt, and three cousins.

"We thought we might do one of these trips instead," Bob replied. "We've been to the beach every year."

"But if we don't go to the beach, I won't get to see Grandma before I leave for college," Kelly said.

"And we couldn't go sailing with Patrick and Kevin," Kelly's brother added. "It's my year to sail the boat too."

"We only get to see our cousins once a year," Kelly continued. "If we go to New York or camping or anywhere else, we won't get to see them at all this year."

"So you would rather go back to the beach than anywhere else for your vacation?" Bob asked. The children nodded yes.

Bob and Linda were surprised but pleased. Somehow over the years, without even planning or realizing it, they had established a family tradition that had become ingrained in the lives of their children. Family time had become more important to them than the trip itself.

Prayer
Thank you, God, for the times we serve you through work and for the times we worship you through rest and recreation. Be with us as we are renewed by our time apart so that we might serve you more effectively each day. Amen.

18 ■ Death

The death of a family member or a close friend can come at any time in our lives. However and whenever death comes, we usually are not prepared for it; and we must deal with a multitude of emotions at the time.

Many harsh realities come into play with the death of a loved one. Not only are there deep emotional feelings and spiritual questions about the loss, but also there are many practical arrangements to plan.

There is the notification of family and friends. Difficult as it is to break such news to those close to the loved one, it is something that must be faced. Funeral arrangements must be attended to through working with the funeral home and the church. Family must be involved in the important decision making and in taking care of the immediate fiscal matters. Out-of-town family must be housed. Funerals for loved ones can bring families together or bring out the deep-seated issues. Emotions reign during these times. We either deal with them in a positive manner or a destructive one.

Sometimes family can feel a sense of relief and celebration for a loved one's release from the physical suffering preceding death. Often well-meaning friends talk about the will and providence of God. But death is always difficult because we experience loss and emptiness. We still question why our loved one had to die at this time. Feelings of guilt can arise over things said or not said, things done or not done, and dreams not fulfilled while the person was alive.

However we experience and deal with the death of a loved one, we can always remember them, and by doing so, keep them alive in our hearts. We can tell their stories and describe their good deeds. We can share the positive effects they had on us and others. But most of all, we can celebrate and remember our loved ones by carrying on with life in a way that says how thankful we are for their lives.

■ From Our Faith Roots

Through the life, teachings, death, and resurrection of Jesus, we know that our physical death is not the end. Through Jesus' resurrection, death was conquered. We know that this physical world is not all there is. Through our faith in Jesus, we believe that there is another life, one that is eternal and one that is in union with God.

As the writer of Romans 8:38-39 says, "For I am convinced that neither death, nor life, nor angels, nor rulers, nor things present, nor things to come, nor powers, nor height, nor depth, nor anything else in all creation will be able to separate us from the love of God in Christ Jesus our Lord."

Although it is natural and appropriate that we mourn our loss and greatly miss our friends and family when they die, we can be assured that they are not separated from God. The grieving process is not quick, and it is not without pain. But, just as we trust that our deceased loved ones are with God, we can depend on God's love and care to sustain us through our grief.

■ Things to Do

→ Encourage family members to remember all of the good times they had with the person who has died.

→ Give people time to grieve. Allow personal time away from normal schedules and habits.

→ Encourage the telling of lighthearted stories about the loved one.

→ Collect pictures of the loved one with family members.

→ Seek professional counseling (individual and family) if needed to cope with grief. Talk to your pastor.

→ Request that monetary memorials be given to a cause important to the loved one.

→ Pass on items belonging to the loved one to family members.

→ Remember the important dates in the loved one's life: birthdays, wedding anniversary, date of death.

→ Encourage the church to find specific ways to let others know when there is a death in the congregation.

→ Help congregational members find ways to express their care and concern for those who are grieving.

→ Consider having the funeral in the church instead of a funeral home.

▪ Things to Talk About

→ How would you describe the person who has died?

→ How do you think the person would want to be remembered?

→ What do you miss most about the person?

→ How is the world a better place because *(name)* lived with us?

→ What would you like to say to *(name)* but never got a chance to?

▪ For More Help

→ *To Live Until We Say Goodbye* by Elisabeth Kubler-Ross. Simon & Schuster, 1997.

→ *On Children and Death* by Elisabeth Kubler-Ross. New York: MacMillan Publishing, 1993.

→ *Our Greatest Gift: A Meditation on Dying & Caring* by Henri Nouwen. HarperSan Francisco, 1985.

→ *When Someone Dies* by Sharon Greenlee. Atlanta: Peachtree Publishing, 1992.

→ *Helping Children Grieve* by Theresa Huntley. Minneapolis: Augsburg Press, 1991.

→ *I Had a Friend Named Peter* by Janice Cohn. Morrow Junior Books, Publishers, 1987.

▪ Devotional Moments

Scripture
John 11:25-26

Hymn
"Hymn of Promise"(*United Methodist Hymnal*, No. 707)

A Death in the Family

I'm an only child, and my parents died within five months of each other. Both were in the their eighties, lived in a nursing care facility, and didn't have long periods of suffering prior to their deaths.

As an only child living in a different part of the state, I had the sole responsibility of taking care of all funeral arrangements while dealing with the loss.

Taking care of Dad at the time of Mother's death was hard. Helping him travel to another state for the funeral was very difficult and emotional. Helping him deal with Mother's death upon our return was more difficult. All of the faith issues of death, resurrection, judgment, heaven, and hell came up in conversations with him.

Dad died five months later of lung cancer. We traveled again to another state to bury him beside my mother. The reality that both of my parents were dead finally sank in, and my sorrow threatened to overwhelm me. The details of the arrangements kept me busy as I dealt with the loss. My immediate family and my church family and other friends helped me during this difficult period. I found comfort in knowing that others really cared.

I still have periods of crying and wishing they were here. I remember going through their things in the garage, and the tears come again. These moments of intense emotion and grief often come unexpectedly.

The biggest comforts I have are my memories and my faith. I'm assured that Mom and Dad feel no pain or suffering; they're together in complete communion with God. One day I'll see them again.

The good memories of our lives together overcome the bad. Pictures, personal items, and funny stories help me keep them alive in my heart.

Death is a strange companion to life. It separates us from the people we love, and yet it brings them closer to the Kingdom of God. Death causes us to question God's plan and to ask why. At the same time we ask for God's comfort. With all of the realities, emotions, and questions, death is a part of living.

Prayer

Dear God, we give you thanks for the life of *(name)*. We grieve and hurt because *(name)* is no longer with us. We know that *(name)* is now with you and that you are with us. Help us to go on living a faithful life as a disciple of Jesus Christ, who overcame death. Amen.

19■Blending a Family

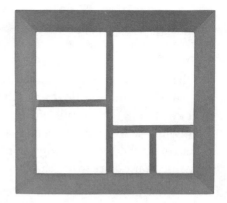

Many dynamics arise when two families come together to create a new family. There are even more things to deal with when new children come into a blended family.

The blended family must begin to take all of the rules, responsibilities, rituals, roles, and traditions of the past separate families and blend them together to create a new family unit. This is not an easy process or one that can be taken lightly. It is hard work to combine the life histories and standards of two different families. In fact, it is nearly impossible to take everything of the past and transfer it to the new family setting.

The age of the children at the time the new family is formed is very important. Usually, younger children adapt more easily. Older children can bring expectations of the way things "should be," based on their previous family experiences. Children already have a number of things to cope with as they grow. If they become a part of a blended family, they face the additional issues of parent/step-parent authority; issues of learning to live, love, and share with other new family members; and issues of establishing new family rules, rituals, and traditions.

Separation and loss are major concerns for many children in blended families. Once these issues are confronted and resolved together, the blended family will be better prepared to handle future difficulties.

■ From Our Faith Roots

One of the greatest stories about how God uses the dynamics (both good and bad) of a blended family features Jacob and his wives Leah and Rachel, their handmaidens, and all of their children. This story is found in Genesis 29-35.

After cheating his brother Esau, Jacob left his home in fear and lived with his uncle Laban in Haran. Jacob became attracted to Laban's younger daughter Rachel and expressed his desire to marry her. Laban required Jacob to work for him for seven years before he would allow the marriage. Jacob was tricked by Laban and ended up married to Leah, the older daughter. Again, Jacob had to serve Laban for another seven years before he could marry Rachel. Even though Jacob loved Rachel more than Leah, Rachel was barren (at first) while Leah had many children by Jacob. In her frustration, Rachel gave her handmaiden, Bilhah, to Jacob so that they might have children. When Leah learned that she could no longer bear children, she gave her handmaiden, Zilpah, to Jacob so that they could have children. By his two wives and their handmaidens, Jacob fathered twelve children. Rachel bore Joseph, who eventually went to Egypt and became the ancestral patriarch of the Hebrews of the Exodus. One of the children of Jacob and Leah was Levi, an ancestor of Moses.

One of the biggest blended families in our Judeo-Christian heritage was used to bring about God's ultimate purpose for God's people. Even through the trickery, deceit, favoritism, jealousy, and anger in this family, God was present with Jacob, Esau, Rachel, Leah, Bilhah, and Zilpah and enabled good to come out of their human frailties. Just as God was present and active then, we can know that God is present and active with blended families today.

■ Things to Do

→ Plan an engagement party that will involve the couple and children from both families working together.

→ Have both families talk separately and together about their feelings, anxieties, and questions about the new family.

→ Consider talking with a professional counselor or your pastor about the potential issues.

→ Help children and adults deal with feelings. (Journaling can be a helpful tool.) Find positive ways to address concerns.

→ Ask your pastor to conduct a house blessing for the new home.

→ Involve all children in the wedding.

→ Share special tokens at the wedding that symbolize the blending of the two families.

→ Recognize that change will not come overnight. Agree to work things out together.

→ Celebrate the new family by doing something special together, such as taking a mini-weekend vacation to a new place.

→ Encourage your church to sponsor a seminar about issues particular to blended families.

→ Remember special dates and occasions that are important to both families and the new blended family.

■ Things to Talk About

→ Will our last names change?

→ What are some things that will not change?

→ What things can we do to help our family get off to a good start?

→ How do we address and work out our conflicts when they arise?

→ What are some things that I really like about this new family?

→ Who will make the "rules" in our new family?

■ For More Help

→ *How to Win as a Stepfamily* by Emily B. Visher and John S. Visher. Brunner/Mazel Publishers, 1991.

→ *Strengthening Stepfamilies* by Elizabeth Einstein and Linda Albert. American Guidance Service Publishers, 1986.

→ *Making It As a Stepparent* by Claire Berman. HarperCollins, 1986.

■ Devotional Moments

Scripture
Genesis 33:4-7

The Blending Begins

Norman and Gayle had been dating for nearly two years. Each had custody of children from previous marriages. Gayle had two daughters, Lisa and Jennifer, and Norman had one son, Jeff. Every once in a while, the subject of marriage came up, but the realities of creating a new family seemed overwhelming. However, as their love continued to grow, they realized that in spite of their fears and uncertainties, they wanted to get married.

With much excitement, they prepared to blend their lifestyles and families. The first thing Norman and Gayle had to do was tell their children. The children had been with each other occasionally and got along fairly well, but they didn't always see eye to eye.

Norman and Gayle decided to break the news at a Saturday night cookout. Everybody was enjoying the evening. After supper they sat down in the den, and Norman and Gayle announced their engagement to the children. They explained why they were getting married and described their hopes and dreams for the new family.

Everything seemed to be going well until, suddenly, Jeff stormed out of the room. Norman quickly followed to see what was wrong. "I don't want to live with those two girls," Jeff explained. "Why do you want to get married again anyway? I thought we were getting along just fine by ourselves," he continued angrily. "Gayle, isn't my mom and those two girls will never be my sisters. How could you do this to me?"

Norman wanted so much for this new family to work out. He was disappointed that his son didn't accept the new situation. Norman loved his son, but he also loved Gayle and her daughters. He wanted all of them to be a family. As he listened to Jeff's anger, he wondered what he should say and do.

If you were Norman, what would you say to Jeff? If you were Gayle, what would you say to Jeff? What would help these two families become a new blended family?

Prayer

God, in the midst of two families coming together to make a new one, be present with all of us. Help us to love each other; help us to understand each other; and help us to seek your guidance when we disagree. As we begin this new family, may your presence be with us, your spirit sustain us, and the love of your son Jesus Christ guide us in all that we do. Amen.

20 ■ The First Home

Purchasing or even renting a place to live can be an adventure. A house is a person's single greatest investment and may well be a first experience at securing a loan from the bank. Such a big step requires careful planning, both in finances and in finding the right house. If the first home involves a move to a different area, additional logistical planning will be necessary. Certainly in the case of a young adult leaving home for the first time, there are emotional issues involved as well.

"Setting up housekeeping" can be exciting and overwhelming. Moving out on one's own requires purchasing or borrowing furniture, appliances, supplies, and utensils to create an entirely separate household. There can be a great deal of expense involved, which is why many young homeowners begin with borrowed furniture, with sheets for curtains, and with an old set of pots and pans from Mom and Dad.

Being on one's own is an event of great life significance. The thought of living apart from parental or educational supervision can be very appealing to most young adults. The responsibilities of paying bills and maintaining the living space can sometimes be a shock that takes the appeal out of independence. Establishing a first home is a rite of passage for most young people. It is establishing an identity separate from one's parents and an opportunity to learn how to live on one's own—things we all must do at some point in our lives.

■ From Our Faith Roots

In Bible times the house, like children, was considered a blessing from God. When the son in the family married, his wife came to live with her husband's family. In this way the family was made stronger, and there were plenty of family members to carry on the father's work. Whether they lived in houses in cities or in the tents of nomadic tribes, the family was a very important element of life.

Houses were simply adorned and utilitarian. Houses were built from mud or stone, had dirt floors and flat roofs. The poorest of homes was a single-room dwelling about ten feet square. It contained one small, high window (located to keep out intruders) and a door that provided entry and light.

The roof of the house served many purposes. It provided a lookout spot, a quiet, cool area where individuals could pray and worship, a place to store and dry crops, and a space to sleep on hot nights.

The interior of the house contained utensils necessary for daily life. Small oil lamps provided light, baskets and clay pots were used for carrying water and food, mats were unrolled for sleeping, and simple dishes used for meals. There was little furniture in the average home. Most of the food preparation and the making of household items, such as baskets and fabrics, were crafted by the women of the household.

Families are a blessing from God. Throughout the Bible we read about people marrying and establishing their own families. Creating new homes and new families ensured the continuation of the lineage and the growth of God's people. It is not difficult to see why the establishment of a new home was a time for celebration and thanksgiving.

■ Things to Do

➔ Plan a housewarming for the new homeowner. Ask guests to bring helpful household items as gifts.

➔ Organize a moving party. Enlist the help of friends, and make the entire event a celebration. After you are settled, invite those who assisted with the move over for a meal.

➔ If you are a parent whose adult child is moving away from home for the first time, send a familiar item from your family home to be placed in the new one. This will serve as a reminder that your families are still connected.

➔ If possible, invest in at least one quality piece of furniture for the new home. This could be a joint gift from several friends or a shared expense with the homeowner.

➔ Encourage your church to celebrate the new homes of members by sharing information about recent moves in Sunday school classes and other small groups.

➔ Create a prayer or litany of blessing for the new home, and send it to the new homeowner.

→ Ask family and friends to share pictures and stories from their first-home experiences.

■ Things to Talk About

→ What is the most exciting thing about your first home?

→ What scares you the most about being a first-time homeowner or renter?

→ Reflect upon your family home. Which things would you like to re-create in your new home?

→ What would you like to be different?

■ For More Help

→ *The Unofficial Guide to Buying Your First Home* by Alan J. Perlis. MacMillan General Reference, 1998.

■ Devotional Moments

Scripture
1 Kings 9:3

Whatever It Was, It Was Home

It was the week after Christmas of 1975. We had only been married a few months when my husband's first job out of college took us to a town far from both our families—a place that was unfamiliar and cold in the gray of December.

Everything we owned fit into the trunk of our car and the back of a U-Haul trailer. As we arrived at the realtor's office, we were excited yet apprehensive about locating a place to live in the unknown surroundings.

The apartment complex that we were referred to was small. The twenty-unit building was located on a secluded corner across the street from a small college. The brick structure was surrounded by a high fence that protected a tiny courtyard and a tarp-covered swimming pool.

The amazing space that would become our home for the next two years consisted of three rooms with ugly, sculptured olive green carpeting, a small bathroom, a galley kitchen in which an open refrigerator door blocked all passage, and one closet. The monthly rent ($145) seemed like a lot to pay for the cramped space, but the apartment was in a nice neighborhood, close to work, and a place where our cat was welcome.

Looking back almost twenty-five years and several homes later, that tiny apartment still holds a powerful, sentimental place in our memories. We remember precisely the way it looked and felt. The round card table covered in flowery contact paper had been a donation from our previous church. The L-shaped brown and orange couch with the sturdy foam cushions had been a hand-me-down from my parents. The one large, walk-in closet held everything we owned—from clothes to linens, from brooms to mops—and was actually larger than the bathroom. The wooden stand that we built to hold a variety of green plants framed the living room window and added a touch of softness to the stark white walls. It wasn't much, but it was home and it was ours.

One of the highlights of our early days of marriage was when a local furniture store conducted a warehouse sale. Somehow we managed to find $100 that we could spend on our first jointly owned piece of furniture. To our delight we were able to buy two end tables for our living room and have enough money left over for a celebration dinner.

As the years passed, we found that it wasn't any of the tangible things that brought happiness to our lives and eventually to the lives of our children. Our *house* wasn't the focus of our lives, but our *home* was. We learned the meaning of the oft quoted adage, "Home is where the heart is."

But there's still something precious about that first place, regardless of the way it looked or where it was located. Remembering our first home takes us back to a simpler, more carefree time when we were laying the foundation for our life together.

Prayer

O Lord, we give thanks to you. We ask your blessing on this house and all who live in it. Fill its rooms with joy and laughter, make it a safe place for all who need shelter and a place of welcome for all who enter its door. Amen.

21 ■ Moving

In earlier times many families lived in the same town and on the same "homestead" for generations. The contemporary Western world is one in which most families move at least once; many families move several times. Our mobile society is influenced by many factors: Economic pressures involving job security, the needs of multi-national employers, and the desire for career promotions all contribute to a society where families frequently move. For others, moving is a guaranteed part of the job or the result of a desire to start fresh in a different place.

Relocating a family can be traumatic. When a family moves, familiar surroundings are sacrificed, close relationships are broken, and culture shock can occur—even if the move is a short distance away. Both processes, leaving and arriving, can be difficult.

Leaving involves packing, selling the house, gathering family records, closing accounts, and saying goodbye. Arriving in the new place presents another list of concerns: the familiar services that were once taken for granted are now gone and must be replaced. New stores, new medical providers, new auto mechanics, and new schools must be found. Even the simplest of tasks, like getting your hair cut, can become difficult in the new community. Careful planning can help families reduce the stresses of a move.

Moving involves a grieving process. Intentional efforts to make a smooth transition to the new home will help but not erase the emotions involved. Relationships will change after the move. Finding ways to build positive experiences for all involved will help make the move less traumatic.

■ From Our Faith Roots

Moving is a common occurrence in the Bible. The early Hebrews were a semi-nomadic people who moved their homesteads to follow their flocks or plant their crops.

In Genesis 11 Abraham moves with his father, wife, nephew, and other household members from Ur to Haran. From there God told Abraham to move "to a place I will show you" (Genesis 12:1). Eventually Abraham settles in Canaan, and God's promise to make him the father of nations is fulfilled.

Abraham moved primarily because he was obeying God, but he moved for economic reasons as well. He was a shepherd who needed to move to find water and grass for his flocks to thrive. Perhaps the biblical reasons for moving are not so far removed from ours today.

We are told of Joseph and Mary moving at least twice, from Bethlehem where Jesus was born to Egypt to escape from King Herod. Years later they moved back to their own home in Nazareth. As an adult, Jesus left his home in Nazareth for Jerusalem. We also have accounts of his ministry in the region of Galilee, where he stayed at the home of Peter in Capernaum. An itinerant preacher, Jesus was familiar with transition and indeed was on the move throughout his ministry.

Moving today may take a great leap of faith on the part of all family members, but God provides courage and comfort. The move from one location to another may be what makes a family survive. Maintaining one's faith in the process of upheaval can be the thing that actually holds the family together.

■ Things to Do

→ Create a litany for a house blessing of your new residence.

→ Create a going-forth litany for the home you are leaving.

→ Make a video or scrapbook of your past house and new house.

→ Leave a note or letter for the new tenant of your house.

→ Ask your pastor to write a letter of introduction to a church in your new community.

→ Allow children to see prospective houses, either in person or through photographs or videos, before the move takes place.

→ If possible, allow children to select the decor for their bedrooms.

→ Have a farewell party with friends. Record their addresses, and give them cards listing your new address.

→ Visit the new community before the move is finalized to help children understand that the new city has many of the same features as the community they are leaving.

→ Read together stories that involve moving, such as the "Little House" books by Laura Ingalls Wilder.

■ Things to Talk About

→ What is important to you as we look for a new house?

→ Define "home" as opposed to "house."

→ List three positive things about moving to a new community.

→ What are the specific times we can plan to visit our old community and neighborhood?

→ What resolutions can we make for our new home to make it even better than the last?

→ What are your greatest fears about moving?

■ For More Help

→ *Celebrating Families* by Lawrence and Diana Osborn. Nashville: Abingdon, 1995.

→ *Mister Rogers Talks with Parents* by Fred Rogers. Milwaukee: Hal Leonard Corp., 1993.

■ Devotional Moments

Scripture
Revelation 21:5a; Psalm 118:24

A Day of New Beginnings

Life was comfortable. Our children were happy. We had a house and friends we loved. Then the signs began to appear: a restructuring of the staff, a shift in priorities, the phasing out of my husband's job.

Fortunately, the work transition would take a year, so there was ample time to search out the available jobs in our area. Seven months into the search, it became evident that there were no churches in the area in need of Rick's talents. I'll never forget the day he came home and announced that he was interviewing for a job at the other end of the state.

"It will be a long commute," I said half heartedly. We had lived in our community since our older child was three months old. Our younger daughter had been born there. The thought of uprooting our children made a knot tighten in my stomach, and the tears came. We prayed diligently for God to guide us in this difficult time, knowing that even the best of transitions would be traumatic for each of us.

The job across the state became a firm and very good offer. In his wisdom and love for his family, my husband agreed to accept the new postion only if the rest of us felt good about the new church and the new community.

We were nervous and somewhat negative during the weekend we visited what was to become our new city.

The new church was huge but beautiful. It had a strong youth program that appealed to our eighth grader. It also had a craft room with a pottery wheel and kiln, which delighted our artistic daughter. The people we met were warm and welcoming. We began the return trip in silence, each of us lost in our own thoughts about the future. Our older daughter finally spoke. "We could do it," she said.

"I don't want to but if we have to, we can do it," her sister agreed.

As moving day approached and leaving friends became an increasingly difficult anticipation, one of our neighbors came by with a proposal. Her two daughters were supposed to spend the week with their grandparents, who happened to live near our new home. She asked if the girls could travel with us, spend the night, and be picked up by their grandparents the next day.

Her offer turned out to be just the transition our girls needed. When they moved, they would have two of their closest friends going with them, at least for the weekend. The first few weeks in our new home turned out to be as difficult as we had expected. But the initial transition was made easier by our children's friends, a happy send off from our church friends, and a warm welcome from our receiving church. Together, with emotional, physical, and spiritual support from those we loved, our family was sent forth to our new beginning and our new home.

Prayer for a New Beginning

God of our beginnings and God of endings, we remember and celebrate all that we have shared together in this place. We ask your guidance, your strength, and your love as we go to our new home. Give us courage to face new beginnings. Give us hope for making new friends. Give us peace in knowing that wherever we go, you will be with us, making all things new. Amen.

22 ■ Retirement

Retirement is when employment from one's job or career permanently ends. It may be mandatory or by choice, but in either case it signals a major transition in a person's life.

As people approach the second half of their working careers, many dream of the day they will retire and have more leisure time. However, for a person who has worked all of his or her adult life, the routine of not having a specific job to go to each day can be somewhat disconcerting after a few months. Many retirees feel unproductive without a schedule of responsibilities to guide their time. To make retirement a happy time, adequate planning in many areas is necessary.

Retirement can be the time to take vacations that were previously impossible to plan. It may also be the time to develop new interests—as individuals, as couples, with friends. For some, the time acquired in retirement may be used to convert the skills from a previous career into volunteer work. For others it may be a time when new skills of the "I-always-wanted-to-do-that" variety are gained.

Careful financial planning is required for a person to be able to enjoy retirement. When the expectation of a regular paycheck ceases, there must be a plan. To live comfortably people may choose or be required to make concessions in living arrangements. "Downsizing" living space is common during retirement years, with many people moving from a large house to smaller accommodations.

Health issues can change a person's plans for retirement. Unexpected health problems can cause not only physical anguish but financial strain as well. Most people will need to consider the potential of health concerns as they plan for their retirement years.

As the baby boomer generation gets older, retirement homes and senior centers will flourish. The mandatory retirement age was once sixty-five. Today, it may vary from workplace to workplace. Many companies faced with downsizing staff will offer attractive early retirement packages to employees. With these opportunities becoming available to younger men and women, the age of retirement for some is slipping back into the fifties. For this reason, retiring from one career may lead the younger person to embark on a second or even third career, making something that was once final now only another temporary choice.

■ From Our Faith Roots

Retirement as inferred in the Bible almost never indicates the end of work altogether. Often it has more to do with physical limitations rather than theological beliefs. In Numbers 8:25 Moses gives specific instructions for the Levites to cease work at age fifty. The reasons were probably more practical than anything else. At the time, the children of Israel were wandering the desert, moving the tabernacle and all of its furnishings as they travelled, which was quite demanding. After age fifty, the Levites were allowed to assist with other duties, including teaching the younger men about the great responsibilities of their positions.

The Old Testament patriarchs appear to have worked in some capacity to unusually old ages. Instead of retiring from family work, we are told about fathers giving more responsibilities to their heirs. When the head of the family died, a son assumed the patriarchal role.

Elderly members of society were revered for the wisdom they could impart to their children and grandchildren. Timothy learned the Christian faith from his grandmother (2 Timothy 1). Moses taught the children of Israel from his vast experiences with God (Deuteronomy 32 and 33). Jacob gave final instructions about the future of his own grandsons to their father, Joseph (Genesis 48).

The years of work and energy required to provide the necessities of life, to raise a family, and to contribute to the community are ways of honoring God late in life. With older age, life is definitely not over. As in the examples in the Bible, productive years may well happen late in life, even up to the time of death.

■ Things to Do

→ Plan a party for the retiree on the day (or near the day) of retirement.

→ Ask your church to offer seminars about planning for retirement.

→ Suggest that your church organize groups and events for senior citizens and active retirees.

➜ Ask family members to write prayers for the retiree.

➜ Encourage grandchildren to collect photographs of the retiree as they recall him or her through the years.

➜ Give the retiree gifts that might help in the transition from full-time work to full time at home.

■ Things to Talk About

➜ What can I expect now that I have retired?

➜ In what ways will I be busier after retirement?

➜ How will life be different if one spouse is retired and the other is not?

➜ What can other family members expect or not expect from the retiree?

➜ What happens if health issues become a problem after retirement?

■ For More Help

➜ *Aging Without Apology* by Robert E. Seymour. Judson Press, 1995.

➜ *Fifty to Forever* by Hugh Downs. Nashville: Thomas Nelson Publishers, 1994.

■ Devotional Moments

Scripture
Ecclesiastes 3:1

An End and A Beginning

Jane and Bob are two people who have figured out how to retire and how to do it right. They met for the first time late in life, a little over a year after Bob's wife had died. Bob had recently retired from his job and had three grown children and two grandchildren.

Jane was a school teacher. Having survived a divorce many years earlier, she lived alone but not far from her grown son and several close friends. It was one of those friends who invited her to a Bible study one Wednesday night. It was at the Bible study that she met Bob. A year later they were married.

Jane continued to work as an elementary guidance counselor after their marriage. In a year's time she was considering early retirement so that she could enjoy more time with Bob. Such a move required careful thought and planning, particularly about finances and insurance.

The couple learned that their combined pensions and investments would provide a comfortable income for their retirement. Jane learned that transferring Bob to her insurance before she retired would provide comprehensive lifelong coverage. With the personal business in order, Jane decided to retire at the end of the approaching school year.

When she retired, the couple's adventure truly began: regular weekend trips to visit the grandchildren; semi-annual trips to visit other children and relatives; cruises with friends; enjoying all the things that they had worked so hard to make possible for so many years.

Retirement for Jane and Bob brought not only fun but also adjustments. Minor health problems plagued both, but they were prepared with adequate insurance and savings. Adjustments in schedules were required, but they enjoyed being together for longer periods.

Some six years into marriage and four years into retirement, they seem to have found a pace that works for them. Each day begins with separate activities and routines: bicycling and swimming for Bob and a local spa for Jane. Noon finds them at their apartment preparing for afternoon errands, with a stop to their favorite restaurant for lunch. Evenings are spent with friends or at their church, where both are active in the life of their congregation.

After a volunteer experience in a mail order project for Bob's son-in-law, Jane and Bob found themselves back on a payroll. They say they haven't really come out of retirement for this work; they just do it to pay for their next adventure.

They describe their philosophy of retirement as, "Tomorrow is your future, regardless of your age." For Jane and Bob, the end of one part of their lives was the wonderful beginning of another.

Prayer

Creating God, who plans for all seasons of our lives, we give thanks for your many gifts in our lives. We ask that your love, care, and ever-present strength be with us as we begin a new chapter of our lives and face the many joys and challenges it brings. Amen.

23 ■ Ongoing Illness

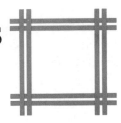

An ongoing illness is a physical or mental disease that requires constant medical monitoring and necessitates adjustments in the home to accommodate the one who is ill. Such an illness may affect people of any age and may be physical or mental in nature.

The significance of living with a person who has an ongoing illness is great for all involved. Changing lifestyles within a home can be difficult under the best of circumstances, but changing physical accommodations for a person who requires medical equipment can be especially disruptive to the entire household. For those who cannot accomodate the patient at home, making arrangements for care in a health facility can be just as difficult. Also involved may be the conflicting issues of what the family really wants and what is best for the person who is ill.

If the illness is terminal, each person must become reconciled to that fact. For adults who watch loved ones struggle with terminal illnesses, the stages of grief may actually begin during the illness, as the physical or mental abilities of the patient diminish. For many people, coping with these changes may be more difficult than dealing with the eventual death.

Children add another dimension to living with people who are ill. The inquisitive and honest nature of children sometimes leads them to ask tough questions. Answers may be beyond their understanding. Sensitive adults will recognize that children need to be informed simply and honestly about what is taking place with the family member who is ill. If possible find tangible ways that children can help. Remember that the presence of a child can often bring hope, courage, and joy to the patient—as well as to the caregiver.

■ From Our Faith Roots

We can infer from scriptural accounts of healing ministries that biblical families dealt with ongoing illnesses. In Matthew 9 we read many stories of Jesus healing people: the paralytic, the blind men, the mute demoniac, and the woman who suffered from hemorraghing. There is a possibility that all of these illnesses were ongoing until they were cured by Jesus.

We believe that God created a good world and that God's will for all people is a good life. With the gift of free will comes the consequences of choices that may be bad for our health. Mental health can certainly affect physical health. The opposite is also true.

Our faith plays an important role in coping with illness. In Matthew 9:20-22 Jesus healed the woman with the "blood issue" (a hemorraghing problem). The woman touched the hem of Jesus' cloak, and Jesus asked her why. Her reply is a declaration of faith: She believed with all her heart that Jesus' healing power could make her well. Jesus replied that her faith had made her well. Our faith sustains us spiritually, if not physically, through ongoing illnesses. If we begin to think of ourselves as spiritual beings existing in a physical body instead of physical beings who try to be spiritual, we can know that the healing power of God cures far more than the unhealthy body. Even when the physical cannot be healed, the soul can be made complete through Christ.

■ Things to Do

→ Encourage your church to form support groups for people living with ongoing illnesses. The groups should deal with specific concerns, such as a group for people with aging parents or for family members coping with an Alzheimer's patient.

→ Form groups to pray for those in your congregation dealing with an illness in the family.

→ Recruit church members to provide temporary respite care for family caregivers.

→ Suggest ways children and youth in your church might minister to those who are ill.

→ Ask your pastor for tapes of worship that can be shared with people unable to attend church.

■ Things to Talk About

→ How will the illness that is affecting our family change our regular pattern of everyday life?

→ What are some specific things each family member can do to help make things run more smoothly at home?

→ What is the most difficult part of living with this illness? Consider this question in light of the entire household.

→ What steps should we take to assure the best living environment for the person who is ill?

■ For More Help

→ *Children of a Certain Age* by Vivian E. Greenberg. New York: The Free Press, 1994.

→ *Til Death Do Us Part* by Jeanette C. Lauer and Robert H. Lauer. New York: Harrington Park Press, 1986.

→ *When You Are Living with an Illness That Is Not Your Own* by Ron DelBene and Mary and Herb Montgomery. Nashville: Upper Room Books, 1992.

→ *Living with Dying* by George L. Harper Jr. Grand Rapids: Eerdmans Press, 1992.

■ Devotional Moments

Scripture
Psalm 57:1b

The Family's Choice

Bill and Mary Ann lived near the heart of the city for half of their married life. When they were in their early forties, they were offered a once-in-a-lifetime real estate deal. Not only did they decide to build a new home but Mary Ann's parents, who were eager to spend their retirement near their children and grandchildren, bought the lot next door. Mary Ann's children were happy about the prospect of having Gran and Grampa next door.

Their dream home was all they had hoped it would be. It was large enough to include an unfinished apartment just off to the side of the kitchen. Separated from the house by a laundry room, the apartment would someday be completed as a guest suite.

Mary Ann's parents delayed building their house for several reasons. As they progressed in years and experienced minor health problems, their house plans were set aside. Their hope of building a new home next to their children was permanently shelved when Gran was diagnosed with Alzheimer's.

The family realized Gran would need constant care and supervision, and her needs would become greater as time went by. For almost a year Grampa managed to care for himself and his wife at their home in the city. But as Gran began to slip further and further from reality, he could no longer handle the situation alone.

At first they considered a nearby retirement home. Gran and Grampa could share an apartment and retain the privacy they valued so highly. But after a few months it was clear that they were both unhappy. The only alternative was to move into the unfinished apartment in Bill and Mary Ann's home.

Adjustments had to be made to the apartment to accommodate full-time residents. When Grampa could no longer watch Gran himself, round-the-clock care was needed.

Weighing the pros and cons of the situation, Mary Ann decided to quit her job so she could care for her parents. The cost of hiring a helper each day was more than her salary. The logical solution was to take on the responsibility herself.

The lifestyle of Bill and Mary Ann's home was radically altered. Their children, now in high school and college, felt the pressure of change. The oldest child transferred to a local college so that she could help with her grandmother's care.

Living with an Alzheimer's patient is trying for this family, but they have learned to face it with a sense of family, a sense of history, and a sense of humor.

Accepting the disease for what it is and what it has done to their loved one and making the best of what remains a stressful situation, keeps this family together and helps them realize that they have made the right choice.

Prayer

Loving God, give us the strength to make decisions that are difficult, the wisdom to realize what we cannot change, and the courage to do what must be done out of love for those we treasure most. Amen.

24■Breaking Up Housekeeping

When an older couple or an individual completely end all duties and responsibilities related to maintaining and living in a house, an apartment, or a condominium, they are said to be "breaking up housekeeping." Often it involves a move into a retirement home, a nursing facility, or a family member's home where someone else cares for all of the things previously handled by the individuals.

It is a time when people relinquish the things that have been a part of their everyday lives, such as cooking, home maintenance and repair, cleaning, and other things associated with living independently.

Breaking up housekeeping can be very traumatic, but some view it with relief. For those accustomed to making their own decisions and being on their own, the need for help in the most basic necessities of life can erode self-confidence and feelings of self-worth.

If you are an adult child helping an older parent with this process, you are affected too. The home you grew up in will no longer be connected with your parents. You may have to take the responsibility of selling the house and making decisions about the contents. The once strong and self-reliant parents are now in your care.

■ From Our Faith Roots

After living in Egypt for many years and generations, the Hebrew people "broke up housekeeping" and set out on a journey (under the leadership of someone they questioned) to an unknown land. Many times as they traveled to their new "residence," the Hebrews resisted and wanted to return to their homes. For this group of people, moving to a new place and to a new way of life was difficult. There were many unknown factors about the move. They could not take everything they owned. They often travelled through frightening surroundings, and the journey was very hard.

All of these feelings and characteristics are similar to those people experience today as they move from a lifelong home. Things are different. Things are scary, unfamiliar, and sometimes difficult. All that has been secure, familiar, and comfortable is abandoned. People going through this transition can never return to the former way of life.

Even when we leave all that is familiar and comfortable and go to new and (on first appearance) strange places, God goes with us. God is in the middle of the process of change, even if we are not aware of it. Sometimes we do not see all that God has in store for us during the times of transition and change. But like the Hebrews, we need to trust God in all that we do, even if that means we have to leave familiar settings.

■ Things to Do

- → Share funny, sad, and meaningful stories that are connected with the family home you are leaving.
- → Recognize that you cannot take everything with you. Take the time to make thoughtful choices about the things you wish to keep.
- → Encourage family members to express what has held meaning for them and what they wish to keep.
- → Talk with friends and family about your feelings.
- → Think positively about and celebrate the things you will give up.
- → Identify some things that will be better after the move. Have some things to look forward to in the new setting.
- → Be sure to take pictures of your last house with you so that you can remember it and tell stories about your former life.

■ Things to Talk About

- → What are the essential things to do as we prepare for this move?
- → How can each family member help in this transition?
- → What will be different in the new arrangement?

→ How does each family member feel about this transition? Can we identify and discuss our feelings?

→ What items from our house have special meaning to the family and to individual members? What do we want to save?

→ How do we determine where our give-away items go?

■ For More Help

→ *And Not One Bird Stopped Singing: Coping with Transition and Loss in Aging* by Doris Moreland Jones. Upper Room Books, 1997.

■ Devotional Moments

Scripture
Ecclesiastes 2:1-6

The Last Move

Mom and Dad broke up housekeeping in 1987. They were moving out of their house in one state and moving to a nursing home facility in another. They had lived in the same house for twenty-five years. Dad only had five more years left on the mortgage payments. They didn't want to move. They wanted to stay in the house, but their health and life situation didn't permit that option.

My wife and I took the week of Thanksgiving to help them sort through all of the stuff in the house. Room by room and box by box, we went through all of the memories that were part of their lives and mine. It was fun to discover old items and pictures. It was rich to share stories that brought back memories. The experience of going through all of the things in the house was fun yet very painful.

Mom and Dad were giving up things that were meaningful to them. They were not only giving up material things but also some of their independence, some of their dreams, and some of their health. Mom and Dad couldn't do many of the things they once did.

The car and house were sold. Furniture and some clothes were given to charities. Decisions were made about what furniture they would take with them. A lot of stuff was just thrown away.

The day came when we left the house, the neighborhood, and the state, knowing that they would never return. The word "never" is so big and powerful when put in this context.

Mom and Dad arrived at their new residence with a good out-look. However, things were different and unfamiliar. Routines weren't the same. To complicate matters, Dad was unhappy, and Mom developed health problems. Life went on, but it was forever changed for my parents.

As my parents added the closing period to one of the last chapters of their lives, they began a new "paragraph" that brought them some joy and relief. Mom's health got a little better, while Dad didn't have to worry so much about the details of life. They got to see their son, daughter-in-law, and grandchildren a lot more than before. They received great joy from being closer to family.

For my parents, this transition was both a blessing and a curse. It robbed them of so many of the things that they felt were important: independence, financial stability, and pride. But it brought much peace and joy to their latter years, provided good care, and allowed more time with family. To begin something new, one must end something. The process of ending and beginning is a continual part of life.

Prayer

Dear God, we give you thanks for all of the good years and memories we have had in this place. We also thank you for being with us during the rough times. As you have been with us in the past and in the present, go with us and sustain us in the future. As you went with the children of Israel through the wilderness into the Promised Land, go with us now into this new situation. Bless us with your presence, your peace, and your guiding hand. Amen.

25▪The Loss of a Home

When a family loses a home, due to financial or other reasons, they lose a part of their identity, their dreams, and their hopes for the future. In cases where the home has been in the family for more than one generation, there is an accompanying loss of family heritage and a loss of the dream of passing the home on to the next generation.

Usually the loss of a home is a negative experience, and all family members will be affected. Spouses often realize that mistakes have been made, consequences will have to be faced, and lifestyles will change. Even when no one is responsible for the loss, people always ask "why" and "why me?" There is plenty of blame to go around—as well as anger, denial, and depression.

Children think about what will happen to their family and where they will live. When they see the effects of strain on their parents, the children may wonder if a divorce may also occur.

The loss of a home brings the loss of friends, neighbors, and everyday rituals. Besides the house itself, there is also a loss of a way of life.

Even though it is hard to predict and face, losing a home can be endured. Making wise decisions, not overextending financial obligations, being aware of present economic and community conditions, and facing change (as hard as that may be) are ways of coping with the loss.

Few families may face this challenge, and even fewer make contingency plans for such a loss. However, a family should think realistically and honestly about the situation. Consider the hurdles of asking for help when it is needed. Think about the needed changes to bring about healing and wholeness within the family.

■ From Our Faith Roots

Job lost just about everything he had, including his personal property and the property of his extended family. He lost much of his material wealth, and he lost his health. Job did not understand why this was happening to him, and he was angry at God. His friends tried to tell Job that the calamities happened because he had sinned against God. Even his wife told Job to curse God and die. Throughout the turmoils and feelings of anger, Job never lost faith in God—even though he had reason to doubt.

Job, in losing much of what he had, was angry, perplexed, frightened, and faithful—all at the same time. He wanted to ask God about the situation. Even when his "friends" offered their explanations of why bad things were happening, Job remained faithful to God.

When people lose something as important as a home, they have many of the same feelings as Job. Sometimes we get angry about our losses and cry out to God. Regardless of our feelings and reactions, God will be with us. It is not God's will that bad things happen to us. As Christians we profess that God is present in the midst of our pain and discouragement.

■ Things to Do

→ Take special mementos from the previous home to the new home.

→ Talk with your pastor about the loss and your feelings.

→ Keep a journal to record your feelings.

→ Schedule a time for family members to discuss their feelings. Use that time to keep everyone informed of what is going on.

→ Find creative and safe ways to express your anger and frustrations.

→ Try to stay connected with friends, and let them know of your needs during this difficult time.

→ Discuss with family members of all ages what they can do to help during this time.

→ Let your Sunday school class or other small group know about your situation and needs. Let them include you in their prayers.

■ Things to Talk About

→ What caused this to happen? Did we have any control over the situation?

→ How can we help each other survive this major transition?

→ What things will change during this loss and transition?

→ How can we constructively express our anger and frustrations?

→ What are our priorities during this transition?

→ Who can help us through this situation?

→ How does our faith in God help during a time like this?

■ For More Help

→ *Filling the Void: Six Steps from Loss to Fulfillment* by Dorothy Bullitt. Dorthy Bullitt Management Services, Inc., 1996.

■ Devotional Moments

Scripture
Psalms 34:17-18

The Last Move

Paul and Sandra had lived on their farm for almost twenty-five years. Paul's father had grown up and lived on the same farm for almost sixty years. Paul's grandfather had bought the 450-acre farm at the turn of the century. Most of the family history of this century was centered around the farm and farm life. It had been passed through three generations, and with each generation came more memories and family stories. Not only was the family story tied to this farm but also much of the family finances and savings.

Bad weather and the decline of the livestock market in 1994 dealt a harsh blow to the family. They lost much of their livestock during the brutal winter; cattle prices went down drastically; and the planting was off schedule because of the excessively rainy spring.

The family had outstanding bills from the previous year and expenses for the upcoming planting. Sandra's bout with pneumonia resulted in major medical expenses. College tuition for their sons added to the financial woes. The bills kept coming. The only answer was a hard one: Sell the farm, and try something else.

This decision meant selling the house, the barn, all of the farm equipment, and all of the land. Much thought and prayer went into the decision that would end a way of life for the family, one that had been a part of their history for nearly a century. Paul felt that he had let his father and grandfather down. He felt that he could have done more and been better prepared for the difficult seasons. Paul blamed himself. At times the feelings of loss and guilt were overwhelming. Occasionally, Paul would try to convince himself that the next year would be better. But he knew what had to be done.

Paul and Sandra sold the family farm in September. They had one last big summer party for their neighbors and family. They remembered the good times, cried over the sad times, and asked for God's guidance in the difficult days ahead. Things would never be the same. A major chapter in the family story had ended.

But it wasn't the end for Paul and Sandra. They took the money from the sale of the farm, paid off the bills, put some away for college tuition, and moved to the city. With the continuous support of their friends, church members, and their pastor, they were able to get through the transition.

Yes, there are scars. It took Paul almost a year of counseling to get through his anger and guilt. It was also hard for him to face his father and talk with him about the farm. They had to give up many of the things they enjoyed about living on a farm and adapt to urban life. Paul found another job in the city. Sandra began teaching in a local daycare school. Their sons didn't miss the hard farm life as much as their parents thought they would.

Paul and Sandra realize that the grief they've experienced isn't that different from the grief of losing a family member. They know they will continue to mourn their loss. However, they have also discovered that their love for one another and their faith will endure in whatever situation arises.

Prayer

God, help me to face the decisions that I must make. Support me when I stumble, listen to me when I cry, and walk with me through the valleys. Even in my frustrations, guilt, and anger, I know that you are with me and will sustain and strengthen me. Amen.

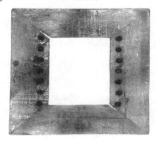

26 ▪ The Loss of a Job

During their working careers, many people will face the loss of a job. The consequences can be far reaching. The first consequence is financial—how to find the resources to meet life's needs. Expenses that were once manageable may suddenly become major obstacles.

The second consequence relates to finding another job that will bring support and personal satisfaction. Sometimes people find that they must acquire new job skills to be considered for employment. Others discover that they are considered overqualified for the jobs that are available. For people who have been employed for a long time, the prospect of "starting at the bottom" seems daunting. However, a job loss can also create an opportunity to try something new and explore new interests.

The third (and sometimes the most significant) consequence of losing a job is the loss of self-esteem and confidence. Individuals often wonder, "Why was I the one let go? Why did this happen to me? What's wrong with me?" Even if the job loss is due to circumstances completely beyond the individual's control, feelings of guilt and inadequacy arise. For many people their identities are closely linked to their occupations. Therefore, losing a job calls into question their self-worth and value as a person. Realizing that we are all loved children of God, regardless of our job status, is an important task for people who have defined themselves by their professions.

▪ From Our Faith Roots

In Joshua 1:1-10 we read God's commission to Joshua as the new leader of the Hebrew people. We can imagine that Joshua must have doubted his abilities to step into an unfamiliar role. However, God gave him a powerful command, "Be strong and courageous; do not be frightened or dismayed, for the Lord your God is with you wherever you go" (Joshua 1:9).

The God that was with Joshua is also with us. God knows our feelings, fears, and weaknesses. God is present even before we take our first steps. God does not abandon us, even in the worst circumstances. God uses the talents we have to help us face issues. As in the story of Joshua, God goes with and before us in whatever we have to face.

In Mark 1:16-20 we read about the call of Peter, Andrew, James, and John. These men went from being full-time fishermen to being full-time disciples. At that time of change did they know God's plan for them? Did they know what they were getting into? For whatever reasons, they followed Jesus and their lives were never the same. God's plan was being carried out through their "job change." What a difference they made!

Many times when change comes, we fail to see how it fits into God's plan for our lives. When we feel that our lives have been turned upside down, it is hard to trust that, "All things work together for good for those who love God" (Romans 8:28). Like Joshua, we can be assured that God can use change for God's purposes.

■ Things to Do

→ Have a family meeting and discuss what this job loss will mean to the family in everyday terms.

→ Discuss how you feel about the job loss with your family or with close friends. Do not hide your feelings; deal with them.

→ Begin to plan specific ways for dealing with the job loss as well as getting another job. "Work" at finding another job.

→ Suggest that your church sponsor a career transition seminar.

→ Take care of your mental health. Consider talking to a counselor or your pastor.

→ Realize that you are not the only person who has lost a job. Many other people go through the same experiences and feelings.

→ Take a skills assessment inventory to discover what you have to offer in the job market.

→ Celebrate with your family and friends when you find another job.

■ Things to Talk About

→ How will the job loss affect our family?

→ What changes will we need to make in our finances, schedules, responsibilities, and general home life?

→ What specific ways can each family member help during this time of transition?

→ How do we (family members) deal with our feelings of anxiety, anger, uncertainty, and fear during these times?

→ What strengths do we possess to help in this difficult time?

■ For More Help

→ *Transitions: Making Sense of Life's Changes* by William Bridges. Addison-Wesley Publishing Co., 1980.

→ *Managing Transitions: Making the Most of Change* by William Bridges. Addison-Wesley Publishing Co., 1991.

→ *Job Shift* by William Bridges. Addison-Wesley Publishing Co., 1995.

→ *Finding Work Without Losing Heart* by William J. Byron. S.J. Adams Publishing, 1995.

→ *What Color Is Your Parachute?* by Richard Bolles. Ten Speed Press, 1997.

■ Devotional Moments

Scripture
Psalm 16:7-11; 25:4-21; 37:1-11

Moving On

In my career, I've lost two jobs. Once because I was told that it was time for me "to move on." The second time, I was informed that my position was being eliminated. Regardless of the cause, facing the reality of losing a job is never easy.

I asked myself "Why me?" and "What did I do to deserve this?" At times I thought, "This really isn't happening, I'm going to wake up and it will all be a dream." But it was real, and I had to deal with the situation.

Carrying the major financial responsibility for my family, I felt enormous pressure to find another job quickly. I worried about what would happen to my family and what changes we would have to make. As I worried with these important practical matters, I still had to deal with my feelings of anger. I was angry at the people and situations that had caused the job loss. Even though I had done nothing to cause the situation, there were still feelings of "What could I have done differently?" Dealing with the practical matters of losing a job and the emotional feelings all at the same time was overwhelming.

Both of my job changes required a move to another city. This makes a difficult situation even more challenging. The first time I lost my job was soon after my wife and I had bought our first house and had become parents for the first time. We had to move when our daughter was only four months old.

When my second position was eliminated after thirteen years of happy and successful ministry, I was devastated. That job loss was harder. Roots had been established; a second child had come into our family; and we were very happy. We didn't want to move!

After six months of dealing with the second job loss, of finding another job, of realizing that we would be uprooting the family, of coping with tears and frustrations, we settled into our new home in another part of the state. Happily, I can report that positive things have come from the new location and job.

Throughout the years, the two job losses, and the resulting anxieties, I've realized some important things about job loss and life. First, I'm not the only person who has lost a job. Many other people experience the same, and I'm now more sympathetic to the problems they face. Second, people need to deal with a job loss and work quickly to improve the situation. Third, and most important, don't leave God out of the process. You never know what God has in store for you. God cares for you, wants the best for you, and will be with you throughout the whole mess. When you can't see around the next corner, God can; and God has some wonderful surprises waiting for you.

Prayer
God, when I am afraid, grant me courage; when I am tired, grant me strength; and when I fear the future, give me hope. Amen.

Leader's Guide

**Suggestions for using *Capture the Moment*
in small groups, Sunday school classes,
retreats, and other church settings.**

Our Christian faith and life events intersect constantly. The
church should help people recognize, celebrate, and discuss these
life events in a supportive Christian fellowship. As we explore
(and we discuss with others) our life and our faith, we are better
able to "capture the moment," learn from it, and grow in our
own Christian discipleship.

Even though this book is primarily designed to be used by
families and individuals within families, it also can be used in
other church settings. Since it deals with connecting life events
and issues with the Christian faith, it is appropriate to consider
using *Capture the Moment* in a teaching–learning setting.

This section is designed to help people use *Capture the
Moment* as a small group study, a short-term study for Sunday
school classes, or as a theme for a retreat. Intended primarily as
a study for adults, *Capture the Moment* can be adapted for use
with older youth.

This guide provides a model for leading sessions using
Capture the Moment as the study resource. The leader will need
to adapt the model provided to meet the needs of the particular
setting and audience. In most cases a group will not cover all
twenty-six life events that are discussed in *Capture the Moment*.
Select the topics that seem most appropriate for the group.

Sunday School Class Setting
(45-60 minutes)

This resource can be used in a six-to-eight-week study in an adult Sunday school class. Most classes will not need to discuss all of the chapters. The class and leader may wish to select several topics of importance to class members. This study will work best in a group that uses small group discussion and some written activities as a part of the learning experience. This study is not intended for a lecture format.

Any adult member of the class with leadership experience can guide these sessions. The leader should be comfortable in a presentation/discussion format; he or she should be able to help the class explore and find meaning in significant life events without defining a "right or wrong" way.

The leader should thoughtfully prepare to make the sessions informative, stimulating, and participatory. The leader should also be flexible enough to allow for "relevant tangents" to happen in the class. As adults discuss significant life events, other important topics for discussion may surface.

■ Suggested Class Format

Preparing to Teach

1. Select life events for study.
2. Read the corresponding chapters from *Capture the Moment*.
3. Read the Scripture passages mentioned in the chapter.
4. Gather any available resources from the section "For More Help."
5. Pray for God's guidance in leading this study.

Teaching the Lesson

There are five helpful steps in preparing a lesson outline for this book. However, these steps are general enough to be adapted to any topic and any group: (1) Get the Group's Attention; (2) Introduce the Topic (sometimes these two steps can be combined in creative ways); (3) Explore the Topic; (4) Respond to the Topic; and (5) Close the Session.

This general outline will be used as we explore a typical class session using one or more of the topics featured in *Capture the*

Moment. Times listed for each part of the lesson plan are only suggestions. Adapt these times to fit the needs of the class.

1. Get the Group's Attention (5 minutes)

Think of a way to immediately gain the interest of your class. For example: On newsprint or markerboard write, "Death is a part of life. What really matters is how we deal with it." Let class members ponder these words as they get settled in the classroom.

If you are doing the session about moving, decorate the room with boxes. If the topic is milestone birthdays, have a birthday cake with banners or balloons in front of the class or around the room.

2. Introduce the Topic (5-10 minutes)

In this step you will help class members begin to think about the relevance of the topic to their own lives. If studying the chapter about death, ask the class members to write their own epitaphs, or list things that concern them about death, or tell about their first experience with the death of a loved one, friend, or pet. Often issues and questions are raised during this time that will need to be dealt with later in the class.

If the session is about vacations, ask people to turn to their neighbors and discuss what they enjoy about vacations. If your next session is about marriage, ask class members to bring pictures from their weddings, or ask class members to describe the funniest thing that happened on their wedding day.

3. Explore the Topic (10-15 minutes)

Present the material from the introduction of the chapter and from the section "From Our Faith Roots." If class members have read the chapter before coming to class, ask them what they remember from the reading. If class members have not read the chapter beforehand, give a short presentation to cover the key points.

"For More Help" in each chapter lists other helpful resources related to the topic. If the leader has had an opportunity to review these resources, he or she may wish to summarize their contents for the class.

Capture the Moment is designed to initiate conversation about important issues. Depending upon the time available and the interest of the class, members may want to do more reading and research about the subject being discussed, or they may want to schedule other classes for exploring the issues in more depth.

4. Respond to the Topic (15-20 minutes)

Ask class members to review and discuss the things suggested in the sections "Things to Do" and "Things to Talk About." These are not exhaustive lists but are intended to stimulate thought about how participants can "capture the moments" in their lives. Encourage class members to make other suggestions about things they currently do or would like to do to celebrate life events. While the items in the section "Things to Talk About" are primarily intended for family and individual reflection, many of the questions provide good material for class discussion. Large classes may be divided into smaller discussion groups. These groups can report what they gleaned from their conversations to the entire class.

Other questions that may be helpful are:

→ Do you agree or disagree with the presented material?

→ How does the Christian faith and the Bible help you deal with this issue?

→ What pressures and expectations exist in our culture about this subject? How do we deal with these?

→ Are there other questions or concerns that you still have about this issue?

As suggested before, you may wish to divide the class into small groups to discuss these and to report back to the entire class. Do not expect everyone to speak. Encourage people to say only what they are comfortable telling. The discussion may raise other issues to be addressed in other sessions.

5. Close the Session (5 minutes)

Use the "Devotional Moments" at the end of each chapter.

Short-term Study
(60-90 minutes per session)

Capture the Moment can also be used as a study for groups desiring more time than the traditional Sunday school hour and for groups desiring to involve other people from the congregation. These could be parent support groups, Wednesday or Sunday evening elective studies, or a home study with members from a particular neighborhood.

Unlike a Sunday school class, members of these groups may or may not know each other. They may come from different levels of participation in a church or may not even belong to the church sponsoring the study. It is important for the leader to be aware of these dynamics. Some of the same planning and teaching methods used in the Sunday school format can be used or adapted to fit this setting. However, there are some things that this type of study offers that the Sunday school hour does not. Specifically, the leader can spend more time on a topic, sometimes spending several sessions on a subject if desired.

Leadership for such a study can come from within or beyond the membership of the church. Once a group has decided to offer a short-term study based on *Capture the Moment*, it needs to recruit primary leadership, schedule the time for the study, and advertise it to the congregation or other selected audiences, such as parents of children and youth. Similar to the Sunday school setting, this study should run for six to eight weeks, with the opportunity to go longer if the group desires to do so.

■ Suggested Format

Preparing for the Study

1. Sponsoring group selects leaders(s) for the study.
2. Decide on the duration of the study. Select dates and times.
3. Advertise the study in the congregation or to a particular target audience.
4. Select an appropriate space to have the study.
5. If the study is elective, determine the minimum number of participants needed.
6. Order copies of *Capture the Moment* for each participant.

Preparing to Lead

1. Select some life events to begin the study, but be open to the desires of the group concerning other life events in the book.
2. Read the entire book to become familiar with all of the chapters. Other resources listed in the various chapters may also be read.
3. Gather resources for teaching, and prepare the first session plan. Be open to adjusting the plan after the first session to accommodate the dynamics and composition of the group.

Leading the Session

The five steps of teaching a Sunday school class (p. 114) can be used in this setting. However, the steps need to be adapted to the group dynamics, especially if members do not know each other and are coming together solely for the study. Below is a suggested session plan for a small group elective study. Listed time limits for each part are merely suggestions. Adjust them to meet the needs of your group.

1. Get the Group's Attention (5-10 minutes)

Create a learning space that is conducive to group interaction. Set up the room in a comfortable arrangement, with tables and chairs sitting in a square or a semi-circle. Provide nametags and light refreshments, if appropriate. Have copies of *Capture the Moment* available for people to review as they wait for the class to begin.

As the study progresses, the leader should arrange the room and materials so that the participants can focus on the session as soon as they enter the room. (See suggested methodology in the Sunday school section.)

2. Introduce the Topic and Participants (10-15 minutes)

Introduce yourself and ask the participants to introduce themselves. A creative way to do this is to ask participants to tell about a recent significant life event they have experienced after they give their name. Or, arrange the class in pairs and ask each pair to ask their partner's name, family configuration, and one important life event from the last five to ten years. Then ask each participant to introduce his or her partner, describing briefly what they have learned.

Give an overview of the study. Announce the topic for the day. Allow time for the group to select topics for future lessons.

Introduce the topic of the first session by using some of the methods in the Sunday school lesson plan. It is important that this first lesson be as inclusive as possible since you may not know the make-up of the group in advance. Death, milestone birthdays, or graduation are good general topics with which to begin. This part of the lesson plan will take longer during the first session because of the necessary introductions to the study and introductions of the participants.

3. Explore the Topic (20-30 minutes)

Information about the topic can be presented in a variety of ways: View a relevant video. Invite a guest speaker from outside the church who has expertise in the topic. A panel of three or four people could be invited to address a topic. The leader can make a short presentation.

It is important to focus on the biblical and theological background for each topic. The participants may want to look up the related Bible passages and discuss how the passages can lead to an understanding of the life event in terms of our faith.

Regardless of the methodology, it is important that the leader provide an opportunity for the participants to gain insight about how to recognize, celebrate, and relate their Christian faith and significant life events. Suggest looking at life events through new lenses and interpreting experiences from these new perspectives.

4. Respond to the Topic (20-30 minutes)

Participants need time to respond to and discuss the material presented. Small group discussion is one of the most effective methods. Groups of three or four people are considered a more comfortable number for interaction. This format also deters the more vocal individuals from dominating the discussion.

One of the best ways to encourage groups to talk is to give them specific questions to discuss or activities that relate to the material presented. Think about the questions or activities in advance, and have all of the necessary items available for people to participate. (See sample of questions in Sunday school lesson plan.) Allow an appropriate amount of time for individuals to complete the questions or activities. Then allow time for discussion in the small group.

Questions in the "Things to Talk About" section can provide catalysts for group discussion. Discuss ways of incorporating the ideas in the "Things to Do" section into family life. Ask participants to list ways the church can reinforce these significant life events, celebrate them in worship, or help people cope with them.

Once the small groups have had significant time to respond to and discuss the subject, call the groups back together to report the things learned. Do not expect everyone to speak. Do not be intimidated by silence. Give people time to collect their thoughts. Always affirm the contributions that each person makes to the whole group.

5. Close the Session (5-10 minutes)

Sum up the ideas, discussions, and the relationship of the life event to the Christian faith. Re-state important points made in the study session. Review implications for daily life, and challenge the group to put the things they have learned into practice.

Use the "Devotional Moments" at the end of the chapter to bring closure to the session.

Retreat Setting
(Two days)

A retreat setting allows a lot of flexibility and creativity for using *Capture the Moment*. The format suggested here is for a weekend retreat, beginning on Friday evening and ending at Sunday noon. It includes an introductory session, four sessions on specific life events, and a closing worship event. It assumes a setting that allows for large and small group sessions, as well as lodging and meals for participants. Choose a setting that provides opportunities for other activities, such as walking, relaxing, table games, and conversation, and so forth. Many churches have retreat facilities within a short (one to two hours) driving distance. This model could easily be adapted to be conducted at a church, with participants coming only during the day.

Decisions need to be made before the retreat, including one about the retreat's focus (the four life events). The composition of the group will provide clues for the selection of topics. A retreat for parents with young children could focus on "Becoming a Parent," "Baptism," "School," and "First-Time Events." If the audience is single young adults, possibilities include "The First Job," "The First Home," "Moving," and "Significant Accomplishments." If the group is very diverse, consider events that are common to all people. Suggested session topics with common appeal might be: "Vacations," "The First Home," "Death," "The First Job," "Milestone Birthdays," "Graduation," "Baptism," and "Confirmation."

The length of the sessions and the type of activities during the sessions will depend upon the age level of the participants. If it is a family retreat with adults, youth, and children, plan activities and formats that involve all ages. The sessions and activities need to be intergenerational. If the retreat is for adults (such as a Sunday school class, couples, singles, and so forth), different formats and activities can be considered. Whatever format is chosen, there should be adequate time within the schedule for four or five sessions, meals, fellowship periods, planned recreation, worship, and free time. Adaptations can be made, depending on the local church, retreat setting, and leadership.

■ Introductory Session: (60-75 minutes)

Since many people will be traveling to the retreat setting after work on Friday evening, the first session should be shorter than the rest and should be used to introduce the retreat's theme. People are usually tired when they arrive, and few arrive at the same time. The first session should begin after most or all of the participants have arrived.

The same five teaching steps suggested in the previous settings can be adapted for the first and other sessions. (See p. 114.)

1. Get the Group's Attention (5-15 minutes)

Ask participants to write down the important events of their lives or in the lives of their families. Give some examples from your own life. Mention things from your distant past to most recent events. Divide the participants into small groups, and ask them to use their lists of events to introduce themselves to the other participants. Have the groups list the life events on pieces of newsprint or posterboard.

2. Introduce the Theme (10-15 minutes)

Bring the entire group back together. Explain that during the retreat, participants will consider life events and explore how we can recognize, celebrate, and interpret these events in light of our Christian faith. Name the four life events to be studied during the retreat.

Describe the schedule for the weekend. Talk about any housekeeping issues.

3. Explore the Topic (15-20 minutes)

If the participants do not already have copies of *Capture the Moment*, pass them out at this time. Give people an opportunity to skim the book. Point out that each chapter consists of a brief description of the life event's significance, reflection on how the event relates to the Bible, suggestions for things to do and things to talk about, and a story or other devotional suggestion that further illuminates the particular event.

Explain that only four life events will be explored in this retreat, but participants can use the book to help them deal with a wide variety of life experiences.

4. Respond to the Topic (15-20 minutes)

Have the participants go back into small groups and look at their list of life events again. Ask the groups to discuss the following questions:

→ Which event is most significant?

→ How did you or your family celebrate or deal with the event?

→ Were you happy with the celebration of the event, or do you wish it had been done differently?

5. Close the Session (5-10 minutes)

Allow a brief time for the small groups to report to the larger class about insights gained. Answer any questions that people have about the schedule for the rest of the retreat.

Close with a prayer of thanksgiving for opportunities to gather as a Christian community, for opportunities to explore important issues, and for opportunities to have fun together.

■ Sessions 2-5 (60-90 minutes)

A typical plan will have a session scheduled for Saturday morning, afternoon, and evening, as well as Sunday morning.

Deal with one life event in each session. The five teaching steps listed in the Sunday school model provide the starting point for the session. However, the setting allows for a variety of methods to be used in the exploration and response sections. Consider using games, storytelling, arts and crafts, guided small group discussion, audio-visuals, roleplay, and other creative methods to help participants explore some aspect of the topic and relate the event to their family and their faith. The activities should be appropriate for the age-levels of the participants. Plan for a balance of activities that involve a variety of learning styles.

If small group discussion/reflection groups are used as the primary response to the topic, select and train the small group leaders so that they are better prepared to help participants reflect on the topics and their experiences.

■ Closing Worship (45-60 minutes)

The closing worship service is typically the last planned activity of the retreat. It seeks to draw all elements of the retreat together in a worship atmosphere. It helps all participants celebrate, reflect, and hear the good news proclaimed in light of their retreat experience together.

This suggested order of worship requires some advanced preparation by the participants during the retreat. This can be done immediately before the worship begins or the evening before the worship service. Modify the order of worship to be appropriate for your group.

Before Worship Begins

Divide the participants into four groups. Assign each group one of the the four life events examined during the retreat. Provide materials for each group to create a paper or cloth banner that focuses on the assigned event. Ask the groups to find passages from Scripture that relate to their topic. Tell them to be prepared to describe how that Scripture relates to their banners.

Order of Worship

Gathering

Have one person from each group carry the group's banner to the front of the worship area as you sing, "This Is a Day of New Beginnings" (*United Methodist Hymnal*, No. 383) or another appropriate hymn.

Praise

Read together Psalm 92:1-4 or another psalm of praise.

Prayer

Give people an opportunity to voice prayers of praise, thanks, petition, and intercession. After each prayer ask the entire group to respond with "Lord, hear our prayer." Pray together the Lord's Prayer.

Proclamation

Ask the groups to read the Scripture they have prepared and explain the relationship of their banner to the Scripture.

Response

Sing "Many Gifts, One Spirit" (*United Methodist Hymnal,* No. 114) or another appropriate hymn. Allow a time for individuals to express how the retreat has been meaningful for them and what new things they intend to do. (Do not require people to speak.)

Sending Forth

As you go back to the daily events of life,
some will be momentous and life changing,
some will be quiet and life sustaining,
some will bring tears and some will bring laughter.
In all, God will be present.